Grunt, Grit and

Grace

Lessons in Leadership From the Dancefloor to the Boardroom

ALLY NITSCHKE

First published in 2023 by Ally Nitschke.

© Ally Nitschke

The moral rights of the author have been asserted.
This book is an Inspirational Book Writers book.

Author: Nitschke, Ally

Title: Grunt, Grit, and Grace: Lessons in Leadership From the Dancefloor to the Boardroom

ISBN: 978-1-4467-1382-2

Editor-in-chief: Anita Saunders
Cover Design: Sarah Rose Graphic Design

Disclaimer:
The material in this publication is of the nature of general professional advice, but it is not intended to provide specific guidance for particular circumstances, and it should not be relied on as the basis for any decision to take action or not take action on any particular matter which it covers. Readers should obtain individual advice from the author where appropriate, before making any such decision. To the maximum extent permitted by law, the author and publisher disclaim all responsibility and liability to any person, arising directly or indirectly from any person taking or not taking action based on the information in this publication.

What Other People Say About Ally Nitschke And Her Work.

★ ★ ★

Ally took us on such a great personal and professional journey. I am beginning a new career and Ally gave me the tools to feel confident and assertive. We learned a lot about our individual personalities and how this can help us be productive and successful in the workplace. Ally was engaging and took the time to get to know us before the course which made it feel personal. I walked out of the classroom each day with my head held high and my confidence boosted. A big thank you. I am no longer afraid to have courageous conversations!

LUCY FELTUS, MANAGER, RSPCA

Ally is a great coach and I feel lucky to have worked with her. She has managed to empower me to go from confused to clear on my future goals and aspirations. She provides great resources, is incredibly encouraging, and knew exactly how to give me the push to go for what I am made for!

DONNA, EMERGING LEADER

I've used services like Ally's before, but she has been the best! She explains things clearly and makes you feel at ease; is professional and knows her stuff. I highly recommend!

TALLORA, BUSINESS OWNER

Ally's coaching allowed me to enhance my influence as a leader not only in my professional life but also in my personal life. Coaching has helped me to master my communication style and uncover blocks to my personal success. If you are willing to look deeply and honestly within yourself so that you can reach your highest potential, then Ally is the perfect guide.

GAYLE KOTHARI, SENIOR LEADER RSPCA SA

The amount of actionable info packed into such a short space of time – Brilliant!

NAT MORLEY, COO KWPX

Thank you, Ally for taking us through your Courageous Leaders program. I have taken many leadership and training programs through the years and none have made me come away feeling more empowered than this one. Ally has a unique way of getting you to engage in the conversation throughout the course and getting you to really see the areas you need to concentrate on. Ally is extremely talented with her training style, keeps you challenging your thoughts and actions while coming to solutions to react and think differently going forward. I felt Ally to be very genuine in her delivery and full of life, she is the kind of person you want to be around. I encourage anyone to take Ally's training, it is one big step forward. I thank you for opening my eyes up again.

JO-ANN MILLIGAN, MANAGER, RSPCA

As I reflect on the past year I wanted to thank you for the impact you had on my leadership journey. I always looked forward to our sessions as it was a time to step back and think about high level leadership and I always came away from the sessions either confirming my approach, getting fresh ideas, looking at things differently, gaining a greater understanding of the situation but generally, together we achieved all of the above mixed in together. Ally's CEO Advisory Boardroom enhanced my leadership so that my whole organisation could benefit. If you're sitting on the fence about working with Ally, say Yes!\

NIGEL MORRIS, CEO Local Government

Ally's professionalism and organisation is second to none. I was really impressed by her ability to tailor the message to the context of our event and ensure its application to the organisational change that was being implemented. Our guests commended your warmth, the pace of your session, and found you engaging and funny.

ALICE CAMERON, DIVISIONAL EXECUTIVE OFFICER,

Ally was our OUTSTANDING MC for the Women in Leadership Summit. From the start Ally was a dream to work with on this summit! She brought enthusiasm, energy and attention to detail to every step of the process - this was even before she stepped foot on the stage. The light and laughter she brought with her to a room full of amazing women leaders left them all inspired, confident and ready to take on the world. I am already excited for the next project we get to collaborate on together. Thank you Ally for being amazing!

EMMA, EVENT PRODUCER

Ally is a dynamic, inspirational speaker on leadership and has now harnessed her time-tested insights, ideas and implementable strategies into this brilliant book. Filled with practical advice you can use to engage better, energise and empower your people as a Leader. It is a must-read!

KEITH ABRAHAM, PASSIONATE PERFORMANCE

Foreword

★ ⭐ ★

"Nothing changes if nothing changes."

Almost 20 years ago I was confronted by a young person who wanted to embark on a new career and make their mark on the world. This was not an unusual situation having hired hundreds of people, but this person was different.

There was a passion and determination that was evident hiding behind her slightly shy and uncertain façade. I agreed to bring her into the team to see if she could release what was inside. After a rocky start stemming from a slight lack of confidence and knowledge, we sat down to talk about her future.

During this conversation, we talked about what had shaped who she was today. How she had faced challenges, showed determination, and achieved so much. We discussed how she needed to harness this and use it to continue to develop her professional career.

There are always obstacles and barriers that exist; it is our choice to keep running into them and keep getting the same result or look for ways to navigate a new path. Our conversation ended with my favourite piece of advice: *"Nothing changes, if nothing changes."*

I am honoured to have been asked by Ally to write this opening for her book. Since the early days in her career, she has grown and taken on all challenges head-on, both in her work and personal life. It has been a privilege to follow her journey and be in a small way a part of it.

In a world constantly evolving, clinging to the familiar can be tempting. We find solace in the routines and structures that have guided us thus far. However, as leaders, we must recognise that true progress requires a willingness to confront the unknown, to challenge the status quo, and to forge ahead fearlessly. It is through this embrace of change that leaders can ignite a flame of inspiration, guiding their teams towards greatness.

Change is the force that shapes who we are and the world we live in. Throughout history, leaders who have recognised the power of change and embraced it wholeheartedly have emerged as the catalysts of progress, reshaping societies, industries, and the very fabric of human existence.

"Nothing changes if nothing changes" encapsulates the truth that growth and innovation are born from a mindset of continual improvement. It reminds us that success is not a destination but a journey. It is a principle that can be used by all, but as leaders, it is our duty to champion this philosophy, fostering an environment that encourages curiosity, adaptability, and the pursuit of new ideas.

Leadership is not solely about reaching the summit; it is about paving the path for others to follow. By fostering a culture that values change, leaders empower their teams to push beyond their limits, challenge assumptions, and redefine what is possible. This allows individuals to discover their untapped potential, and collective efforts give rise to extraordinary achievements.

Change is not always easy; in fact, it can be the hardest thing we do in a day. But if you take on the challenge it will define your vision, courage, resilience, and empathy—and this in turn will allow you to navigate the complexities of change. It will soon embed itself as a mindset and provide you with the "Grunt, Grit, and Grace" to take on any challenge.

As you embark on this journey through the world of transformational leadership, remember that change starts with you. The power to make a difference lies within your hands.

Embrace the discomfort of the unknown, challenge the familiar, and dare to redefine the boundaries of what is possible. By doing so, you will not only inspire those around you but also leave a mark on the future that is created.

So, let us delve into the pages that lie ahead, embarking on a transformative voyage together.

May this exploration ignite the flame of leadership within you and remind you that *"Nothing changes if nothing changes."*

Daniel Crago
Director at DC Consulting

Acknowledgements

— ⋆ ★ ⋆ —

It's not an easy feat writing a book; some say it's a labour of love, I think it's more just labour.

I couldn't do this work without the incredible support of some key players. Jane Anderson, my mentor and coach who is one of the most exceptional people I've ever met. Thank you for challenging my thinking and being the best cheerleader a girl could ask for.

The incredible women in my mastermind, Dr Stacey and Alena, who started out as colleagues and have become friends, thank you for your unwavering support and guidance at any hour, day or night. I'm very glad to have you in my circle.

Big fat thank you to the team at Inspirational Book Writers, Dave Thompson, Davina, and Nicole for holding space to write this book and lending me their belief and faith during the process.

The editing team at IBW, thank you for polishing this up and finessing my words. Having you on the journey is a dream come true.

A huge thank you to my clients, past, present, and future, who are continuing to collectively lift the leadership experience and lead with courage for themselves, their team, and their organisations.

Last but certainly not least, my family. My beautiful mother-in-law, who is so generous, wonderful, and supportive and always helping with the boys whenever I need it. My children, for entertaining themselves so I could get some words on a page, and for being a continual source of inspiration and purpose for doing the things that I do. Special thanks to my eldest Max, who had the flip chart out next to me to keep me on track. "Mummy, where are you on the journey? Can we mark some stuff off?" His support at just eight years old is setting him up to be a remarkable leader one day.

My beautiful husband, Alex, who goes along with my crazy, out-there ideas, supports me more than I could ever summarise, and is the best partner in life a girl could ask for.

Thanks a million, I love ya guts!

Table of Contents

Dedication

★ ★ ★

To the most special people in my life: Alex,
your unwavering support knows no bounds.

My tiny people; Maxi, Harvey, Theo, and Eddy,
you are my sunshine, my love, my light.

Introduction

It's interesting when writing a book because you go through a process of *"Oh my gosh, who the heck am I to be writing about this?"* to *"Oh my goodness, this is actually quite good"* to *"Oh my goodness, I reckon this is really going to hit the spot for people who read it."* And then full circle again.

What's also interesting is that when it came time to write this introduction, I realised that I very rarely actually read the introductions in the books that I read for my own enjoyment, development, and learning. As I was reflecting on this, I realised, actually, this is my exact approach to life. Jump into the deep end. Sink or swim. Fake it till you make it. And dig in.

If this resonates for you, perhaps you're someone who also gets a lot done in a short amount of time. You're probably also someone who is a high achiever or a high performer, and it's my belief that that's actually what life is all about. Making the most of what's available to us, in the time that we have here on earth.

♣ ♣ ♣

When I was 16 years old, I lost my Dad to cancer. This was a time before there was much awareness of the horrible disease that cancer is. Dad was my biggest cheerleader; he believed I could do anything I set my mind to. Having someone continually cheering for you in your corner can spur on some amazing things. Equally, when that person is no longer there, there's a big hole to either fill or fall into. At age sixteen, I had a decision to make: I could fall in the hole of grief and pity OR I could make the most of this thing called life. Many people don't go through that type of loss until much

1

later in life; at just sixteen, I became acutely aware of the importance of time, how we use it, and the legacy we leave for those we leave behind.

Since then, I have committed to living life to the fullest. My "career" started as a professional ballet dancer; prior to that, I studied full-time dance at the academy, and in the dingy rehearsal studio that we shared with some of the art students. In the communal area, there was a mural on the wall that said, *"Shoot for the moon, even if you miss, you'll land among the stars."* I used to stare at the mural for hours while rehearsing at the barre, hours during breaks in rehearsal, and I'd sometimes stare at it for no reason at all. I have been shooting for the moon since early on in my life, and as a result, I've had some wonderful experiences which I'll share throughout this book.

My career as a professional dancer was cut short due to some art funding cuts, and I quickly found myself jobless and thirsty for work. I walked up the main street of the country town I grew up in to look for a job. Walked into the bakery and asked if I could have a job—nope. I crossed the road to the menswear store—also a no. Stood outside the front door of my local credit union that I'd been banking with for years (thanks, Dad, for the financial literacy!). I walked in and asked for a job and started my career in the corporate world the following week.

For nearly 20 years I've been working as a leader and with leaders in the corporate world, across industries and sectors; it's been quite the learning experience. I've worked with small teams and large teams of over 500 people. I've worked with high-performing teams, and downright toxic teams. I've worked through major change, transitions, and transformation, and I've worked with global organisations.

What I'm obsessed with these days is courage. Not the brave kind, the kind of courage where we lean into the ickiness, the uncomfortableness, to do the things that are hard, and come out the other side better for it.

And I think it comes down to three things: Grunt, Grit, and Grace.

This book is for leaders who are looking to elevate their leadership for the betterment of human connection and the human experience. Interestingly, when I was doing some research for this book, I came across a staggering statistic: only 23% of leaders become leaders because they actually want to lead people. Others step into a leadership role for positioning, status, or income and sometimes it's just the logical next step in their trajectory.

This book is not for those who view leadership as merely a means to an end. If you see leadership solely as a stepping stone for personal gain, whether it's for climbing the corporate ladder, or attaining a higher status, or increasing your income, then this book may not resonate with you. This book is not for individuals who are primarily focused on the material rewards and external recognition that come with a leadership position or title. If your motivation for becoming a leader lacks a genuine desire to connect with and make a positive impact with others, then this is not for you.

It's no secret that leadership is a lifelong learning journey. I'm lucky enough to work with some exceptional leaders. The kind of people who want to be excellent leaders and work with incredible people, not leaders chasing their next salary bandwidth.

I work with leaders who want to have a massive impact and a lasting legacy. I work with the 23% and those striving to join the 23%ers club.

This book is for those 23%ers who are truly committed to what it means to lead people, what it means to lead themselves, and what it means to hold on when things are tough, boring, and downright messy.

From here, you have a choice: Do you want to carry on as you always have? Or Do you want to shoot for the moon? Even if you miss, you'll land among the stars.

I'm known as *"The Courageous Conversations Person."* I was holding an event last year, and as I came off stage, someone asked me, "What's the link between your ballet and Courageous Conversations?" I realised it's the ability to do hard things, it's the ability to keep going when it's uncomfortable, and it's the ability to make it look effortless.

It's the Grunt, Grit, and Grace of ballet, leadership, and life. If you're wanting to be more, do more, and achieve more in your life, in business, for your team and organisation—then you're in the right place.

Let's dive in!

Chapter 1

Why Grunt, Grit, and Grace Is Important

What I'm seeing in the leadership space can only really be described as Leaders Languishing.

It's no surprise that since 2020 the world has changed; in a few short years, we've lived through a pandemic, witnessed a war, and there have been floods and fire. And we're not even talking about the work and the toll this level of crisis has had on leaders, their well-being, and their families.

Adam Grant famously coined the word "Languishing." It aptly explains what leaders (everyone, really) are currently experiencing, and will continue to experience. Languishing is described as "The neglected middle child of mental health."

Adam Grant describes languishing as

"The sense of stagnation and emptiness. It feels as if you're muddling through your days, looking at your life through a foggy windshield."

What I'm noticing is the number of leaders who are ready to dust themselves off and get back into the *people part* of leadership. Enough is enough already of this languishing limbo. I recently read a staggering piece of research on the motivations of leaders and was surprised, but also not surprised to learn that 51% of leaders seek a position of leadership for the monetary gain and another 26% for status. And a meagre 23% seek leadership positions for the purpose of leading people and leaving a legacy.

For those leaders, for those 23%ers, the ones who are deeply committed to honing their craft, the craft of leadership, I think there are three key things they need to embody.

Grunt, Grit and Grace.

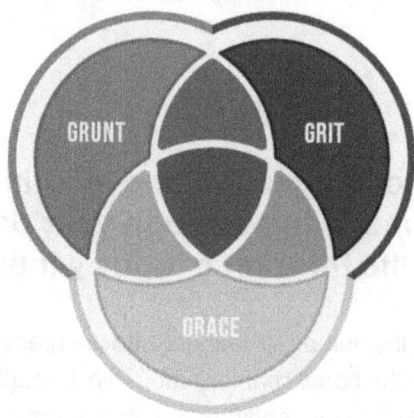

Grunt

You can think of Grunt as the physical and mental work of dancing. It's the learning, the study, and the heavy lifting. For dance, this means learning the positions and the steps. Understanding the moves. Becoming aware of how the body works and how it can be developed to accomplish amazing things.

In leadership, Grunt is much the same. It's the heavy lifting of responsibility. It's learning about yourself, your team, your strategies, and your goals. It's understanding where strengths and weaknesses are, and how to motivate your element of the organisation (yourself and your team) to be better, stronger, and more fluid. It's the foundational work that gives you little to no reward—at least not at first. But it gives you the strength to begin the real practice of leadership.

This is the grunt work of leadership, the heavy lifting, the heavy-duty thinking, the heavy responsibility.

It's hard. As Roosevelt famously said, nothing easy is worth doing.

Grit

Grit, on the other hand, is the practice of leadership. It's no surprise that leadership is hard work. It's putting in the hours. It's learning on the job. It's failing (fast) and moving on. It's being 100% accountable. And it's practice, every single day.

Grit is a little bit like holding on (for dear life). If I think back to my years in the studio and on the stage, grit was the process of falling over and getting up again.

Grit was doing the same step or routine over and over again until it was right and ingrained in our body.

We used to have a saying in the ballet world: *"Learn fifth to forget it."* Fifth position is one way of positioning the feet that any dancer would be able to show you no matter how long they've been off the stage. We practised fifth position so frequently because we needed to be able to do it without thinking about it. We needed to be able to "forget it" or stop thinking about it, so that it became a part of who we were, like breathing. It became muscle memory, where over time you could instinctively *know* your feet were in the right place. And that took Grit.

Grace

Finally, Grace. Grace is the bit that people see. One of the most famous ballets is *Swan Lake*. Swans are often described as graceful and the dancers in *Swan Lake* are required to show that same gracefulness in every one of their moves, whether it's the strongest lift, jump, and pirouette or the smallest wave and flutter of their fingers. But what the audience doesn't see is what's gone on behind the scenes, under the surface.

They don't see the sheer muscle strength required to make a jump and land it perfectly. They don't understand the determination it takes to hold one position and then fall into the next as if it took nothing more than a slight wind to blow the dancer over. Every movement takes hundreds of precise muscle movements and an incredible focus. But because it looks so graceful, sometimes it even looks easy (and that's the point).

Grace in leadership is the same way. It looks easy from the outside, but it's the end result of being supported by incredible foundational work, immense capabilities, and skills obtained through years of practice, sweat, and even tears. But to the audience (your team) it simply looks like being able to take the high road. It looks like being able to let the water flow down your back and carry on despite challenges, setbacks, and failures.

Of course, as the leader you know the truth. But the true benefit of grace is that you feel its benefit, too, though you know that it's the result of all those other elements that came before.

The 23%ers who are able to master these three areas will be setting themselves up for Resilience, Courage, and Brilliance. They're setting themselves up for a beautiful, successful, connected future, and a bright career as a leader.

LESSON 1:

Leadership is a gift, it's an opportunity to better people's lives. It can be challenging and fulfilling, a wild ride. The current statistic of less than 1 in 4 leaders actually wanting to lead people is a problem, and an opportunity.

There are not many who become brilliant, there are even less who are willing to go the distance.

If you're one of the 23%ers know that you're here to make a difference to those you lead.

Chapter 2

The Resilience Factor

★ ★ ★

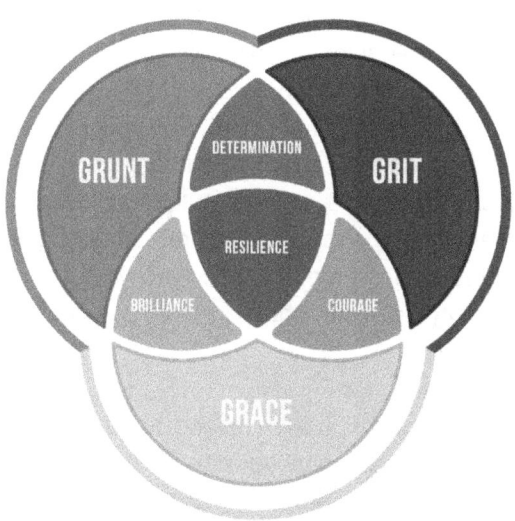

Resilience, at its core, is the ability to bounce back, adapt, and persevere in the face of challenges, setbacks, and adversity. It is the inner strength and mental fortitude that enables individuals to maintain their resolve, overcome obstacles, and continue moving forward towards their goals. Resilience involves a combination of emotional, cognitive, and behaviour factors that contribute to your ability to withstand and thrive in difficult situations and under challenging circumstances.

The resilience factor, grounded in the foundations of determination, brilliance, and courage, encompasses the essential elements that amplify and cultivate resilience in leaders.

Determination, a combination of Grunt and Grit, forms the bedrock of resilience, representing a steadfast commitment to honing your craft (whether that's ballet or leadership), even when faced with setbacks or discouragement. It fuels the resilience factor by driving individuals to persist and take action in the pursuit of their goals.

Brilliance within the resilience factor involves leveraging Grunt and Grace to embody intelligence and creativity, and hone your problem-solving abilities to find better solutions and navigate challenges effectively. It encompasses your capacity to think critically, adapt strategies, and approach situations with agility and resourcefulness.

Courage, another foundation aspect, the intersection of Grace and Grit, is your willingness to face fears, embrace vulnerability, and take calculated risks. It involves stepping out of comfort zones, challenging limiting beliefs, and embracing change and uncertainty. Courage empowers you to confront adversity head-on, knowing that growth and resilience lie on the other side of fear.

By embracing determination, brilliance, and courage, leaders can enhance their resilience factor. They can develop a resilience mindset, cultivate their emotional intelligence, and build a support network while practising self-care to adopt strategies for stress management and problem-solving. The resilience factors, rooted in these foundational elements, empower leaders to navigate life's challenges with strength, adaptability, and a steadfast commitment to their personal and professional growth.

After all, you're learning fifth to forget it.

The Resilience Leadership Ladder

In the world of leadership, where resilience is the key to success, it is key to recognise the connection between the graceful art of ballet and the demanding realm of leadership. Just as ballet dancers progress through different levels of mastery, so too do leaders navigate various stages and roles in their journey towards excellence.

Starting at the beginning of each journey, leaders embark on a new role with optimism and the need for focused attention; moving into level two, they immerse themselves in training and learning, eager to understand their environment and accelerate their progress.

As they reach level three, leaders encounter the demanding grunt work, requiring clarity and decisive action amidst the challenges they face. It is at these critical stages that the resilience really emerges as a necessity, propelling leaders forward towards their goals. This chapter delves into the parallels between ballet and leadership, unravelling the essential principles that enable leaders to thrive and ascent to levels of performance with grace, influence, and lasting impact.

	ACTIVITY	FOCUS	ATTITUDE	RESILIENCE
7	Composure	Excellence	Gratitude	100%
6	Craft	Tenacity	Confidence	75%
5	Commitment	Discipline	Tenacity	50%
4	Clarity	Energy	Focus	20%
3	Effort	Decision	Determination	10%
2	Learning	Practice	Curiosity	-10%
1	Audition	Showing Up	Optimism	-20%

Level 1: Audition

Let's start at the beginning: leaders who are at Level 1 are stepping into a new role or preparing to take on a new role. They're optimistic about what's in front of them, and their focus needs to be on taking action. One step in front of the other. Similar to dancers who are at the beginning of their journey and auditioning for their next "big" part. The hardest (and the easiest) part is showing up. Their attitude throughout this level needs to be optimistic. What is possible?

Level 2: Learning

Leaders at Level 2 are learning; they're still new to their role, and their environment, and they're curious about what's going on around them. They need to be focused on practising their art of leadership to get to Level 3. Their attitude needs to be curious. They are curious about the world around them, their team, and how to be a better leader.

Level 3: Effort

Level 3 leaders are really doing the grunt work at this level. Their focus is on making a decision, THE decision, to knuckle down and put in the effort to become a wonderful leader, or giving into frustration when things get a little tricky or tough.

Perhaps it's longer days, or days filled with heavy-duty thinking. And decision fatigue. Leaders at this level need to embody an attitude of determination.

Level 4: Clarity

Leaders at this level have made the commitment: they've decided leadership really is for them. They are clear on their identity as a leader. They're aware and determined on the work ahead, now their focus is putting in "the work." Their attitude needs to be that of focus. Focus on what's next, focus on what's working, and focus on what they're going to do to move the needle.

Level 5: Commitment

Level 5 leaders are at the commitment level, the grit level. They're white-knuckling, holding on, while also repeating things and building that muscle memory. They're actively committing to improvements, they're tenacious in their approach and attitude. Their focus is on their discipline.

Level 6: Craft

Level 6 leaders are seeing the fruits of their labour. They're tenacious in their leadership approach, they're confident in their abilities to lead, and they're finessing their craft and identifying what works for them, and what doesn't. There's still work to do, but it's easier and they're moving into flow.

Level 7: Composure

Leaders at this level are full of grace, they're calm under pressure, considered, great at listening, and able to prioritise easily and seamlessly. Their focus is on leadership excellence. These leaders make it look easy. They are influential and leave an impact. It's important to recognise that leaders at this level didn't get here overnight. They practise an attitude of gratitude and relish the success of those around them.

As a leader you must embrace the journey of growth, knowing that each level holds its own significance and learnings and opportunities for development. By embodying the qualities of optimism, curiosity, determination, focus, commitment, craftsmanship, and composure you can elevate your leadership and leave a lasting impact on those you lead.

I hope this chapter has prompted your thinking; it serves as a reminder of the importance of embracing each stage of your leadership journey and the resilience needed to overcome challenges along your journey. Keep striving, keep growing, and embrace the transformative power of leadership.

LESSON 2:

There's a saying that Success leaves clues. When we reflect on what has given us results in the past often we can replicate those future results.

For me, it's always been Grunt, Grit and Grace.

What is it for you?

Chapter 3

People Don't Become the Best Magically!

————— ★ ★ ★ —————

**"It takes 10 years to become an
overnight success."
Jeff Bezos**

You may have heard that it takes 10 years to become an overnight success.

Early days in the beginning of starting my leadership consulting practice —
Made For More — I was completely overwhelmed, and almost paralysed by
how slowly things were moving and how much I just didn't know. Someone
very wise reminded me:

**"Don't compare your beginning with
someone else's middle."**

It was of course exactly what I'd been doing. Comparing and comparison.

It's rare that you have the insight and the inside word on someone's
complete journey. We only ever really see the tip of the iceberg, and
what people are willing to share. Even in today's campaign for #hashtag
authenticity, there's still a level of what people see, and what they *want*
you to see.

Everyone's life is curated.

What's happening on the outside is very rarely the whole truth (and nothing but the truth). When I think about some of the best leaders globally and those I'm privileged enough to work with, there's one thing in common and that's that none of them happened overnight.

Becoming the best doesn't happen magically, or even accidentally. It happens with a decision. With a clear sense of purpose and the conviction that everything you're striving for is within your reach … you just have to reach out for it.

The Power of Well-Placed Focus

Early in my career, I was working for a wonderful organisation in banking and finance. I'd managed to get a few runs on the board and was building a name for myself. One lunch break, I went outside and was reflecting on what I wanted to achieve in the next six months. I'd been goal-setting since before I even knew what it was. I still clearly remember sitting on that park bench in 2004 and writing an extensive list; some things were short-term goals, others longer.

When I finished my lunch break, I decided that I was going to have the best year in my career yet, and I built the "yes" strategy. I was working as a lender at that time, and while sitting there, I figured out that if I said yes to every single enquiry that came in, regardless of if I was busy, I'd have more conversations, and build my knowledge and network. And ultimately close more deals.

It worked; in 2005 (and 2006) I was sales star of the year for the whole organisation. Amazing what a little bit of strategy and grit can do.

1% Improvement: The Bike Riders

I'm always fascinated by performance, especially high performance. How is it that some individuals succeed, and others, well, don't?

I wanted to share a remarkable story about the British cycling team. Full disclosure—I don't cycle, and I'm not British. What I do know is that there are always lessons to be learned.

In 2003 the British cycling team hired a new performance director, David Brailsford. The cycling team had a long history of not performing well, and Brailsford was brought in to change things. His approach, which he called "the aggregation of marginal gains," would revolutionise the team's performance and ultimate success.

Brailsford's philosophy was simple yet profound: seek small, incremental improvement in every aspect of cycling. He believed that by enhancing each element by just 1%, the cumulative effect would lead to significant overall progress. From the outset, Brailsford and his coaches made seemingly minor adjustments. They optimised bike seats for comfort, applied alcohol to tyres for better grip, and trialled heated-over shorts (think hoodie shorts, but for sports performance) and biofeedback sensors to maximise performance—all tiny, and relatively easy-to-understand changes.

But they didn't stop there. Brailsford and the team delved into previously unexplored territories, uncovering additional 1% gains. They experimented with massage gels, and learned optimal handwashing techniques from head medical staff to reduce the likelihood of riders picking up the flu. They engaged a sleep specialist to identify individual ideal pillows and mattresses so riders had the best chance for quality sleep. They even painted the inside of the team truck white to detect minute particles that could affect bike performance.

These marginal gains, though seemingly small on their own, accumulated to extraordinary outcomes. Within five years the British cycling team stunned the world by securing 60% of the gold medals in road and track cycling at the 2008 Beijing Olympics. They continued their winning performance in the 2012 London Olympics, setting numerous records.

Over a remarkable decade, British cyclists achieved an unprecedented 17 world championships and an astounding five Tour de France victories. The secret to their success lay in the relentless pursuit of marginal gains, and of course handwashing is always important.

This story raises intriguing questions: How did these seemingly small improvements yield such monumental results? How can we apply this approach to our own lives? The power of marginal gains lies in their cumulative impact and their ability to unlock untapped potential. By embracing the mindset of continuous improvement and seeking tiny advancements in various areas, we too can experience remarkable transformations. Let the lessons of the British cycling team inspire us to uncover our own marginal gains and unleash the extraordinary within.

The Power of Tiny Gains

1% better everyday 1.01^{365} = 37.78

1% worst everyday 0.99^{365} = 0.03

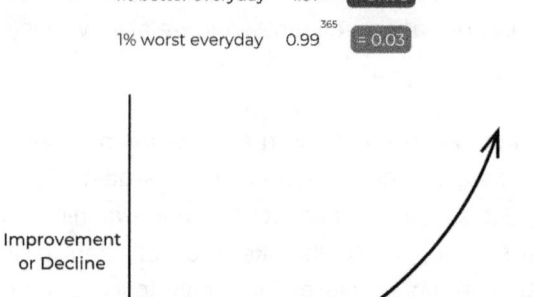

Improvement or Decline

1

1 Year

LESSON 3:
Just improve one thing every day.

You might be wondering how you could possibly implement something like this for your organisation, and while you may not have the ability (or reason) to paint the inside of a truck white, there's ample opportunity to apply marginal gains in the corporate world.

The first place you could look when applying the marginal gains approach is to have a look at the ways you could remove friction. We unpack friction in Chapter 11: Friction and Fire.

Chapter 4

Awaken Your Excellence

Excellence is a funny thing. I see people who lean into it and seek it out. And I see others who actively shy away from excellence as though it's taboo to want to be excellent at something.

I think sometimes excellence is confused with perfection. To be clear, I'm not talking about perfection. I'm talking about building your skills and honing your craft as a leader to become brilliant.

I believe that everyone has the potential to be good, great even. Great at something in their own right.

What I see happen time and time again is people giving up when the going gets tough.

For every person who's exceptional at what they do, they've pushed through the barrier of hard to move into excellence.

As someone who has spent their life being a high achiever and a high performer, I get it. There's that special something about being at the top of your game, setting your sights on something, and achieving it. Equally, it can also be ostracising and intimidating to others who don't have that same drive, and don't understand why you would continually push yourself rather than rest on your laurels.

If you're a high performer or a high achiever, you'll know what I mean. If you're striving to become a high performer and high achiever, you'll need to really commit to excellence for brilliance's sake!

All that effort and determination that goes unseen is setting you up for your future success. I used to be ashamed of being excellent at what I did. I was taught from a young age that being good at something was "attention seeking." As a young child I entered my first ballet competition, and the first year I received an honourable mention. I was so shocked I tripped over as I stepped forward to curtsy, and then I cried my eyes out and with the stage lights couldn't find my way off the stage through my blurry vision. The second year, I worked hard in class and during rehearsals. I didn't know it at the time, but before each lesson I set the intention of what I was going to work on in the name of excellence each and every time.

When it got close to the competition, I wasn't confident. In fact I confided with my friend Phoebe that if I didn't get at least an honourable mention this year, I was going to hang up my shoes. I'd worked so hard, I thought if I didn't get a mention then ballet perhaps wasn't for me.

That year I didn't get an honourable mention. I won.

I was completely blown away; I had no idea that was going to happen. I'd hoped to get an honourable mention, and walked away with a medal. It was my first real taste of success. I'd spent the year working at the barre in preparation for pushing myself to the limit in each class, and the effort, discipline, and determination really paid off.

After the competition I walked out of the dressing room and into the foyer of the theatre where the parents were waiting for their children. I was met with squeals of laughter, and congratulations, everyone was very excited for me. It was a weird feeling; I didn't know how to accept their kind words.

I walked up to my mum and overheard her talking to another mother who was quite literally gushing about how proud she must be. Mum said, "It's actually rather embarrassing, to be honest." She saw me, gave me a nod, and off we walked to the car. We didn't talk about that success, or what it meant. I was taught early on that to be successful, to win, to be at the top of your game is embarrassing, and self-indulgent.

It set a fire in me to be even better, to try harder. I developed a "well, I'll show you" attitude that was effective, but probably not particularly healthy.

Perhaps you had a childhood that was rewarded with winning or academic success. Perhaps you spent a childhood seeking approval and validation for all of your brilliance too. Whatever your reason, please know that very few people make it to the point of being the best at what they do.

If you truly want it, grab that desire, that passion, your belief by the horns, and strap in. It's a wild ride, and as I like to say, if you don't fall you can't fly. After all, you're shooting for the moon, remember?

"If you don't fall you can't fly."

If your belief is not there yet, please feel free to borrow mine. You can take it all if you need.

Tall Poppies

"We think to small, like the frog at the bottom of the well. He thinks the sky is only as big as the top of the well. If he surfaced, he would have an entirely different view."
Mao Zedong

In the vibrant tapestry of human accomplishment, there's this thing called Tall Poppy Syndrome that's been hanging around like a shadow. It's a saying that's unique in the Australian and New Zealand Cultures. It's described as this urge we have to snip down those who dare to rise a little higher as if their success is a threat to the rest of us. But seriously, in the pursuit of our dreams and progress, we need to recognise this behaviour for what it is and rise above it, creating a culture that celebrates success instead of squashing it.

Tall Poppy Syndrome might sound fancy, but it is basically the idea that we can't handle someone doing really well. It's like we're allergic to success or something. Maybe it starts when we're kids, being told not to brag about the things we're good at. And sure, it's good to be humble, but it's not helpful when that turns into pretending we're not good at anything. It's like we're cutting off our own wings just to fit in.

Getting rid of this syndrome means changing how we look at success. Instead of seeing it as a threat, we should see it as a kick in the pants to go after our own dreams. When someone does something incredible, they're showing us what's possible. And guess what? Success isn't like a cake where there's only a limited amount. It's more like a buffet that keeps getting bigger – there's plenty for everyone.

We've got to start celebrating wins – big and small. This isn't just for the fancy award shows; it starts at home and in schools. If we encourage kids to do their best and give them high-fives for even the little victories, we're setting up a world where success is cool, not something to hide.

Looking at the bigger picture, places that give a thumbs-up to success tend to do better than those that don't address tall poppy syndrome.

In this world where we're all connected and ideas can go viral in seconds, we can't afford to let Tall Poppy Syndrome hold you back. Progress, of course isn't only a one-person show; it's a team effort. When everyone brings their A-game without fear of getting cut down, that's when the real magic happens.

So here's the deal, let's pull up those roots of Tall Poppy Syndrome. Let's start high-fiving success and cheering on the people who dare to chase their dreams. Imagine a garden of possibilities where every flower gets to stretch and shine without worrying about being snipped down. It's time to stand tall, together, and show the world that celebrating one person's success only makes the whole garden look even more beautiful.

Diamonds Are Made

"A diamond is a chunk of coal that is made good under pressure."
Henry A Kissinger

Pearls are made from irritated Grit over and over again.

Why are we talking about precious gems, you might wonder? Well, I think there's a lot to be learned from the things we value. If leadership was easy, everyone would do it, teams would be happy, and organisations would be thriving. And I'd be out of a job.

No one ever said it was easy; leadership is a life-long journey, of learning, failing, and learning again. In fact, one of my clients in education encourages her team to fail and as a team they call it First Attempt In Learning. Isn't that a wonderful reframe?

"Without challenges, you would never grow.
Push through your challenges. Earn your greatness."
Unknown

Often we give up, just before we have a breakthrough. Whether it's through leadership, communication, or anything that seems hard. For years my non-dancing friends used to ask me if I was nervous about going on stage; for them the idea of performing was anxiety-inducing. I'd often reply that I was actually excited.

Years later I learned that neurologically nervousness (fear) is excitement without the breath. The only difference being how deeply we breathe and the story we tell ourselves. Nervousness as I'm sure you can imagine includes shallow quick breathing. Excitement, on the other hand, is deeper, more steady breathing.

A technique I'd encourage you to try is box breathing; box breathing allows your nervous system to reset. I'd also challenge you to start replacing your own understanding of nerves. If someone asks if you're nervous, respond with, "I'm actually really excited."

How to box breathe

In for 4, hold for 4, out for 4, hold for 4. Then repeat again.

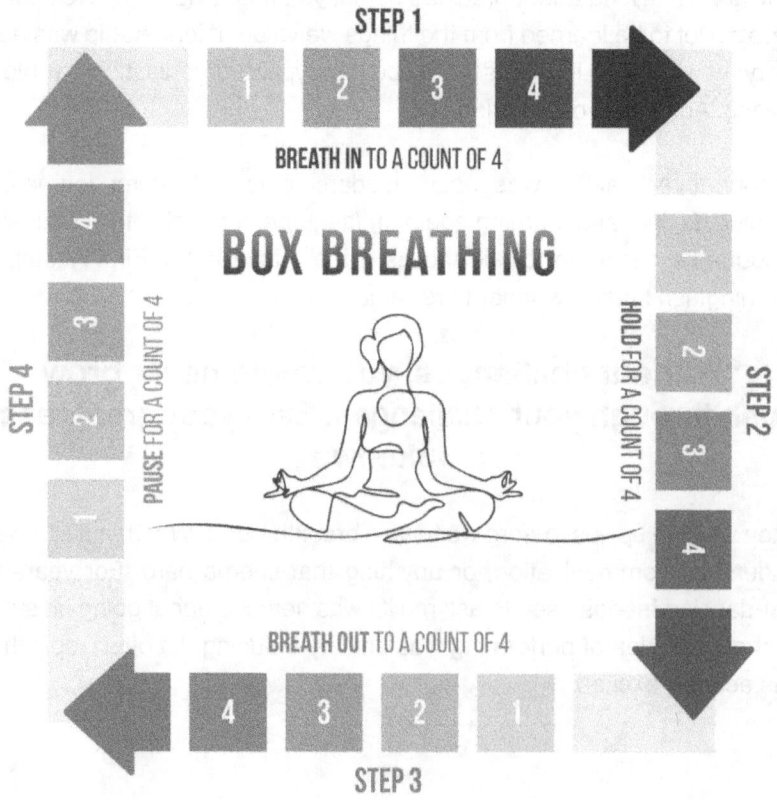

LESSON 4:

Glitter and sequins have a place off the stage, bring some sparkle where ever you go. It's always the right time to shine bright like a diamond.

Shine a light to remove those shadows, And spread those wings and soar.

Act 1:
Grunt and Grind

Cambridge defines Grunt as *a sound or being in the trenches.* And I think this is so true—*to make a short, low sound instead of speaking, usually because of anger or pain, i.e. he hauled himself over the wall, grunting with the effort.*

Make no mistake, Grunt is all about effort. Brilliant leadership takes effort. It's about a commitment to yourself, it's about learning. Learning deep in the trenches. It's the groundwork. It's the continual and committed effort involved.

When I finished school in Year 12 and went to celebrate schoolies, we had a 16-seater bus that we were taking to celebrate. At some stage, while we were painting it, the battery went flat. No worries, I thought, I'll just give us a push start.

And so I did.

The grunt of pushing a bus, all 5'4" of me as a 17-year-old, was confirmation enough that I was strong, and my belief that I could quite literally push a bus was enough to see me through. To this day this is still one of my favourite stories when I question whether I can do something. Well, Ally, remember that time you pushed a bus? You can do this hard thing.

"You need to go through the motions to learn how to do it."

In the ballet world I think about grunt as "throwing a leg over." Putting in the leg work. Doing a step, sequence, or routine over and over (and over) again. You will stumble, of course, it is brand new, but you need to go through the motions to learn how to do it. It's the physical conditioning, as well as the mental conditioning to push through that discomfort. It's the repetition and teaching your body how it feels, and what works, and what doesn't.

Grunt involves going outside your comfort zone. It's the courage piece, leaning into the physical discomfort or perhaps the mental discomfort to keep going.

When people hear the word grunt, it's often associated with grunt work, the physical side of activity. Perhaps it is physical labour, the physical movement of the body for athletes, the grunt if you're working out at a gym (both the noise, grunt, and the effort involved). What each of these things have in common is the conditioning.

Conditioning of the body in this instance, but what I'd like to explore with you further is the conditioning of the mind. For many this comes under the guise of resilience, but I think it's actually grunt; it's conditioning our mind on how we prepare for and respond to the hard stuff.

In my past life as a professional ballet dancer it was the physical movement of putting in the leg work, doing it over and over again. In the early days of learning a new step or routine, you will stumble because it's brand new, and your muscles become fatigued because they're working in a new way. Your mind is continually being challenged to give up, or take it easy. You're breaking new ground; it takes grunt. If you're committed to brilliance, you know the importance of resilience; you continually go through the motions until it becomes easier, and becomes more fluid.

I think back to my early days in leadership, and everything felt a bit stiff and robotic. I would be practising scripts, trying out new tools and techniques. I knew the skills I was learning and trying to adopt were important but I hadn't used them before. They felt awkward.

Over time I adapted to them and they adapted to me. This was things like having courageous conversations, something I'm well known for. It was things like active listening (not as well known about this one). It was often developing my own cadence and flavour on what it meant to be me as a leader. What did leadership feel like to try on? Was it comfy, or was it a bit like a brand-new shoe? This was rolling the legs over, so to speak.

Chapter 5

The Virtues of Grunt

———————— ★ ★ ★ ————————

**"The women whom I love and admire for
their strength and grace did not get that way
because shit worked out. They got that way
because shit went wrong, and they handled it.
They handled it in a thousand different ways on
a thousand different days, but they handled it.
Those women are my superheroes."
Elizabeth Gilbert**

In the realms of ballet and leadership, the virtues of grunt manifest as the pillars of strength and resilience that propel individuals towards greatness. As Elizabeth Gilbert so eloquently stated, it is through handling life's challenges and overcoming obstacles that individuals transform into superheroes.

Grunt, with its connotations of effort, perseverance, and courage, resonate deeply with both the physical and mental conditioning required for ballet, and perhaps are underrepresented and underappreciated conditionings required for leadership too.

When I think about ballet, it's the embodiment of grunt in a dancer's pursuit of brilliance. It is the dedication to countless hours of training, the determination to execute intricate steps flawlessly, and the desire to convey the sheer beauty of movement that drives their journey. Just like a dancer must repeat steps tirelessly, leaders also go through the motions, honing their skills, perfecting their craft, and embracing the discomfort that comes with growth.

Leaders, like ballet dancers, must adapt to new skills and techniques, breaking through initial stiffness and awkwardness to find their unique cadence and identity.

As we explore the virtues of grunt in this chapter, we will uncover the interplay between dedication, determination, and desire in both ballet and leadership. We will witness how these virtues forge resilience, strengthen character, and unleash the untapped potential within. Through the lens of grunt, discover the transformative power of effort, the unwavering commitment to continuous learning, and the relentless pursuit of brilliance.

The Three Ds

Virtues of Grunt

Dedication: The willingness to give a lot of time and energy to something because it is important.

Dedication is a critical aspect of both ballet and leadership. Ballet requires a level of physical and mental discipline to maintain form, technique, and performance.

Likewise, leaders must be dedicated in their decision-making and strategic planning, maintaining focus and keeping their team on track.

In late 2019 Justin Trudeau said, "Change has never before been this fast, and it will never again be this slow."

I think we can say the same for leadership: Leadership has never before been this complex, and it will never again be so simple.

Your success as a leader, a good leader, is dependent on your dedication to be just that. To be one of the 23%ers who is constantly and consistently looking to lead and change the experience of your people.

Determination: The ability to continue trying to do something, although it is very difficult.

Determination is a broader term that encompasses both perseverance and tenacity. It refers specifically to the quality of being resolute and focused on achieving a specific goal, often in the face of significant obstacles or opposition.

Desire: To want something especially strongly.

Desire, the third D when it comes to grunt, represents the burning passion and unwavering longing to achieve something meaningful and impactful. It is the intense yearning that propels leaders forwards, and separates the averages from the greats.

Leaders with a strong desire possess a clear vision of what they want to accomplish and are willing to put in the necessary effort and sacrifices to turn their aspirations into reality. This deep-seated longing fuels their determination and fuels their dedication, providing the motivation and focus needed to overcome obstacles, inspire their people, and navigate the complexities of leadership with unwavering resolve.

In essence, desire acts as the driving force behind a leader's unwavering commitment and their relentless pursuit of excellence.

In Leadership What Does Grunt Actually Mean?

Grunt is the foundational piece to brilliance. I'm lucky to partner with amazing and ambitious organisations and work alongside leaders who are well on the path to brilliance.

Leaders and organisations who are already brilliant, and want to be even brilliant-er. Grunt is for leaders who want to be at the top of their game, and with a little 'luck', some hard work, resilience, and a pinch of strategy, they'll get there.

Turning Over the Legs

In 2010 I had an opportunity to trek the Himalayas; it was brilliant! And in preparation for the 12-day trek, I went into training. I was speaking to an avid marathon walker at my gym one day about the upcoming trek. Aris was in his 60s and had been a walker for a long time. He was the kind of walker who would knock out 100 kms over a weekend, just for fun.

I was speaking with him one day about the upcoming trek, and I asked whether I should put the treadmill on a maximum incline and sweat it out, wear a weighted vest, and do a gazillion squats … what was going to get me "trek fit"? And he gave me the most easy yet profound advice. He said, *"Ally, you just need to get some k's (kilometres) in your legs."* What he was saying was that my legs needed to turn over so many times so that when it came time to the trek, they'd be conditioned with the right technique to walk to the top of the mountain, some 4,000 metres above sea level.

Interestingly, running is said to be our most efficient form of transport. Endurance running has been instrumental in the evolution of humans. There are several thoughts as to how this came to be, the most captivating hypothesis is in relation to persistence hunting. Persistence hunting was used when in pursuit of an animal and chasing the animal until it ran to exhaustion. The pursuit would often take place during the hottest part of the day, and Humans could outrun, or rather persist for longer because of our unique ability to stay cool by sweating.

Over time, we've overcomplicated 'foot transportation' to adapt to modern-day living and convenience. I remember speaking to my Nanna—you may have a story like this too—she went to school in Germany, and in the winter had to wear her skates and ice skate the 40 miles to school and back. Now, I can't for sure validate that it was really 40 miles. I can, however, confirm that I have never had to ice skate, or even walk 40 miles to get to school. In fact, just last week my kids were grizzling about walking home from school (while I carried their bags, mind you) in some drizzle.

Yes, I think we've definitely adapted to comfort and convenience.

I think grunt is a little bit like that; we can all do it (grunt/hard work/effort), and we sometimes make it more complicated than it needs to be.

As a brilliant leader, what can you do to remove the complications, get comfortable being uncomfortable, and just turn the legs over?

LESSON 5:

Don't wait for the right conditions to go for it. I'm sure the hunters who were chasing down their prey for 5-8 hours weren't waiting for the weather to be just right, and have 'their ducks in a row'.

There's some questionable myths to becoming an overnight success. Mostly the fact that it's overnight. So often we see the end product and not what's happened in the lead up. If you're just getting started, don't compare your beginning to someone else's middle.

Win your own game.

Chapter 6

(dis)Comfort and Control

--- ★ ⭐ ★ ---

When it comes to grunt, I think it really comes down to how comfortable you are being uncomfortable. In discomfort, what you can control, and how much effort you can put in.

Understanding the dynamics between control and discomfort, as well as comfort and lack of control, can provide invaluable insights into your own behaviours, attitude, and choices.

Discipline, Discipline, Discipline

Discipline is one of those traits, that's needs to be practiced. It is said that how you do one thing, is how you do all things. I disagree, I think your discipline directly corelates to your desire for growth, in whatever capacity that means for you, combined with a mindset of curiosity and learning.

Essentially—Where discipline exists + curiosity there is an opportunity to lean into discomfort allowing growth to take place.

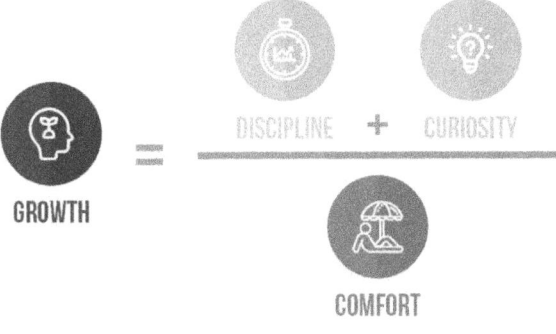

OR, if you prefer, what I like to call The Grunt Formula

The Grunt Formula is really the key ingredients required to get through the 'tough stuff' get through to growth.

In short, what you really want to start to understand is that if your comfort level increases, your opportunity and rate of growth decreases. The more comfortable you become, the harder is it to tolerate discomfort. Often this is where an external factor will force us to move out of comfort and we have the opportunity to change, or to find the next comfy thing. You ability to tolerate and withstand discomfort, will directly impact your ability to withstand growth.

The Art of Impossible

I like to think about grit as the stuff that really defines someone. It's the characteristics that shine through. When someone is between a rock and a hard place, grit is what will get them through—their determination to keep on going, their courage to show up when it feels tough, and to do it anyway.

Throughout 2020 and 2021 we have seen so many leaders who embodied grit, perhaps to their own detriment. In the early days of the pandemic the number of leaders I spoke with who were trying to support their team, unsure about what was coming next and continually putting one foot in front of the other, was staggering.

What they all had in common was the belief and commitment to be there for their teams and families, and to be the best they could be in the circumstances.

Circle of Comfort

"A ship is safe in harbor, that's not what ships are built for."
John A Shedd

There's something pretty nice about staying within our comfort zone. It feels snuggly, it's like wearing your favourite UGG boots with a cuppa tea and a warm blanket. Why on earth would you get out from under there?

Remember earlier in the book I mentioned about being acutely aware of time, and the one life we have to live? That life will pass you by if you stay in your comfort zone?

What I see most often is people recognising that they're comfortable, but being too afraid to leave that nice snuggly bubble.

What I know is that greatness is just on the other side of fear. You were not designed to stay safe, certainly not if you're one of the 23%ers who are leaders because they want to lead people and leave a legacy. Recognising what's on the other side of your fear zone can be enough for you to leave it. Recognising that that discomfort you're feeling is only temporary. Once you bump up against the edges, and push through the mental boundary, on the other side of your fear zone is where the magic happens.

This is the learning zone, this looks like putting your hand up to say yes, even though you might not feel ready.

I over heard my children the other day, the littlest one really wanted to ride a 'big boy' bike without the trainer wheels, but he didn't know how to, and kept falling off. As most tiny people tend to do, He thought he would never be able to ride a bike and was destined to have trainer wheels for ever.

I sat with him and we talked about all the things he had already learned to do so far. And then I share that he hadn't learned how to ride a 'big boy' bike YET.

When we add YET to the end of a sentence, we allow ourselves the opportunity to recognise that the journey isn't over just yet. Adding "yet" to a sentence that might be the key to unlocking expansion and optimism.

These are some of the statements I head from my clients who are doubting themselves and their abilities.

I can't ride a 'big boy' bike.
I'm not ready to do that.
I don't know how to do that.
I can't get this right.
I don't know what I'm doing.
They haven't promoted me.
They haven't replied to me.
I don't know what I should do.
I can't present to the board.
I'm not articulate enough.
I'm not ready.
I'm not a 23%er.

Here are the same statements with a 3 letter word added to the end. When you add 'yet' to your sentences, it means that something you expected hasn't happened... yet.

I can't ride a 'big boy' bike... Yet
I'm not ready to do that... Yet.
I don't know how to do that... Yet.
I can't get this right... Yet
I don't know what I'm doing... Yet
They haven't promoted me... Yet
They haven't replied to me... Yet
I don't know what I should do... Yet
I can't present to the board... Yet
I'm not articulate enough... Yet

I'm not ready… Yet
I'm not a 23%er… Yet

See how differently these land. It leaves the door open for what's yet to come.

Once you lean into that discomfort you move through the learning zone into the sweet spot, the growth zone. This is where we prove all our fears and hesitations wrong. It's taking that leap.

When I was 15 I was cast the lead role in *Cinderella*. There was a really tricky step in the duet that involved me running across the stage, taking a flying split leap, and landing in splits in my partner's hands. There were a lot of things that could go wrong. Jump at the wrong time, not get my legs out in time. Get tangled up in legs and arms and fall over. Not jump high enough and be embarrassed. My partner, who was also the principal dancer said, what would happen if you just nailed it. I considered this for a while and took a few steps back, ran across the stage and leapt (for dear life!), and it was brilliant. Exhilarating. Scary. Was it perfect? Absolutely not, but it was reframing rather than thinking about all the ways something could go wrong.

What if, what if it actually went right?

As humans, we're very good at staying safe, thanks to our amygdala (lizard brain) designed to keep us safe. In our Neanderthal days this was the trigger to run from a sabre-toothed tiger, or fight off another tribe.

Today, we're not at risk of sabre-toothed tigers, and are unlikely to get into a physical fight at work, catching the spiral of all the things that could go wrong and reassuring your lizard brain that you are in fact quite safe. And instead asking what could go right.

Looking at the below model, we can explore the various zones and their corresponding qualities.

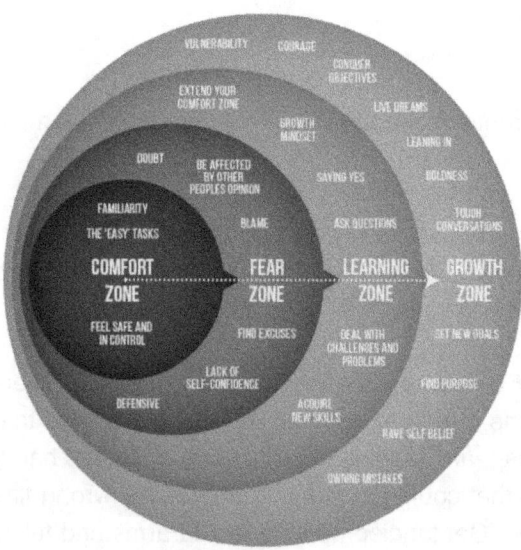

As you can see, staying in the safe zone is comfortable, like wearing a comfy pair of fluffy socks. They're nice, but you're probably not going to see much of the world wearing them.

In the next zone, that's really where people begin to lean into the discomfort, sometimes by choice, often by necessity. The difference between those who continue to grow, and those who don't are the ones who recognise that the uncomfortable ness is just a by-product of what's on the other side, and that's growth.

Leaning Into Discomfort

When you're bumping up against the edges of your comfort zone, it feels uncomfortable. Being okay with being uncomfortable, is the first hurdle to growth and navigating yourself through grunt.

Control

The drive for control can be a two-edged sword. Too much, and we end up being rigid and inflexible. Too little, and life degenerates into tumultuous chaos.

To achieve balance, we need to purposefully control our outlook, stance, and character by engaging helpful activities with people who are supporting and encouraging, have an optimistic mindset, and provide challenging thinking along the way.

There are the more tactical things we can control such as our workflows, inboxes, who and where we work, but I think the most important is to recognise what we can control and what we cannot.

Mindset

I'm often asked where our mindsets come from. By now you've probably heard about the growth mindset and fixed mindset.

But where does a growth mindset or a fixed mindset come from before you learn what it is? Essentially, people's mindsets come from their personal histories of success or failure (regardless of truth, but rather perception and perspective), and their response to those successes and failures. Later on in the book I mention about being told I was lucky. Upon reflection there was an element of luck, but not just luck alone.

When we talk about mindset, much (in fact, most) of our belief systems is formed during our formative years (0–8years). Of course, at that age we don't have the cognitive ability to be able to process and correctly filter how our beliefs are being formed and consequently our mindset.

For example, as a child you may have been praised for your talent rather than your effort which then extends to the belief that if you're not good (enough) then your (self) value diminishes.

Internal Locus of Control

You may have heard about your internal locus of control; if not, let me explain. Everybody has a level of what they can and cannot control. Sometimes we spend too much time trying to control things that are beyond our control, and not enough time focusing on what we can control.

In terms of grunt and resilience, being acutely aware of what you can control and what you can't is paramount if you want to be successful as a leader.

I often think of the lead-a-horse-to-water fable—"You can lead a horse to water, but you can't make it drink."

When you're not able to control something, someone, or a situation, you're the person leading the horse in this instance. You can lead and guide someone (a horse) to water, but you can't physically make someone change (without influence).

As a leader it's important to recognise what you can control and what you can't. Here's an example:

Things You Can Control

Your beliefs
Your attitude
Your patience
How you choose to respond
Your perspective
How kind you are
Who your friends are
How you speak
How many risks you take
How kind you are to yourself

Your boundaries
Whether to ask for help
Whether to offer help
Whether or not you judge others
Whether or not you judge yourself
The self-compassion you demonstrate
Your self-care practices and hygiene
What you listen to
What you read
What you consume on social media

Things You Cannot Control

Other people's beliefs
Other people's attitude
Other people's patience
Other people's behaviour
How others choose to respond
Others' perspective
How kind others are
Who others choose as friends
How others speak
How many risks someone else takes
Other people's boundaries
Whether someone offers to help you
Whether or not others judge you
What others listen to
What others read
What others consume on social media

Taking responsibility for yourself is so important, especially when being a role model.

Personal leadership accountability is an attribute that you want to start instilling in your organisational culture so everyone is responsible for what it is that they're doing and their own results. This reduces the blame game that can happen when something goes wrong.

LESSON 6:

Strength is built by repetition, and repetition, and repetition. Just like going to the gym and building muscle, micro tears have to occur.

For leadership, it's repetition, the micro tears, are getting it wrong, and learning from those occurrences to become stronger and stronger and withstand the discomfort of growth.

Chapter 7

Influence and Intention

You know, it wasn't until I started my own Leadership Consultancy—Made For More—that I really understood the depth, length and breadth I'd been a leader for. Leadership doesn't begin with a role or a title, it's an attitude, and mindset and a belief. I am and have been a leader for over two decades.

Most often leaders are recognised and identify with the title of leader; for other, leadership goes much deeper than that. In my first book, *Rise of the Courageous Leader*, I talk about leadership being an inside-out job; you have to lead yourself before you can lead others.

In the dancing world, I didn't realise at the time (thank goodness) that I was a leader. Because I was a high performer I was one of the best in Australia (fourth in the national competition 1999!) and people looked to me for direction. Sometimes, because I was literally standing front and centre of the room and that's where they were taking their cue. But often for other reasons too. Being good at what you do gives you the ability to influence other people. It's comes with a big responsibility that you can choose to acknowledge and embody.

In leadership, if you're good at what you do, people begin to trust you; once they trust you they begin to connect with you; once you have a connection you're able to influence those around you.

What Is Influence?

Influence is the ability to personally affect the action, decisions, opinions, or thinking of others. It sounds pretty easy but might not be as simple as you think.

Ultimately, influence allows you to get things done and achieve your desired outcomes.

The effect of leading with influence goes beyond your team or your network. You can even influence your whole industry to adopt a radical or innovative idea you've come up with. Better yet, you can be the frontrunner and lead your industry towards a change that will benefit everyone.

The Power of Intention

I was running a women's executive leadership summit and we were talking about the importance of influence. One of the delegates asked what the difference was between influence and manipulation. A brilliant question. I think the difference for true leaders is *intention*.

Is the intention to influence for the greater good, or is it for self-gain and self-advancement? Many of the brilliant leaders I know understand the heavy weight of being influential and are careful to make sure they use their influence for good, rather than evil.

To be influential, people need to trust that you can perform and show up.

"Those who master the art of influence are often skilled at tapping into the emotions that drive people's actions."

To really understand whether you can influence, first let's look at what is happening in the world right now.

To give some context, my eight-year-old and seven-year-old came home from school declaring that when they grow up, they're going to be YouTube influencers.

Say what now?

When I was eight, my prospects were set on being a prima ballerina closely followed by a French teacher (talk about the influence of teachers in early childhood).

The Rise of the Influencer

In this day and age, being an influencer is a legitimate job that pays good money. So, anyone can see that influence is a huge driver behind people's decision-making processes.

Apply this concept to your role as a leader, whether that's in business or within your organisation, and you can see that you also want to be an influential leader.

You want people to work with you and for you. You want them to help you grow, nourish, and expand your business in the direction you want to take. And likewise, you want to help them grow and expand.

Historical vs New Era Leaders

Historically, a leader was an authoritative figure whom people listened to because they were the "boss." Influence and authority came with the title so whatever you said is what people had to do.

We're now seeing that that's not always an effective method of leadership. Although change happens and people do their work, the impact of the leader's influence doesn't carry over a long period.

At the basic level, influence is about compliance. Beyond getting people to do what you want them to do, you want to influence them to want to follow you, offer excellent customer service, and deliver a high quality of work of their own accord.

You do that by making your people intrinsically motivated to do those things.

Which Type of Influential Leader Are You?

If you want to be a truly influential leader, and you want to make a lasting impact, it's going to take some work, and it's going to take some grunt. In John C Maxwell 's 5 levels of leadership, early in a leaders journey, their influence and followers, follow purely based on the individual performance. People like to be around and follow those who are doing well.

You want your influence to extend beyond a project and seep into the behaviour and thoughts of your people so they will be intrinsically motivated to get behind your mission and vision.

One good technique is to show them the personal benefits they will gain by changing their way of thinking or acting. If you don't know how to do this, reach out to me and let's have a courageous conversation about it.

Leadership With Integrity

To lead with integrity requires grunt. It's not always popular to do what is right over what is fast and easy. People will follow if they see you doing the hard yards too. This is a classic walk the talk. Being in the trenches certainly helps when it comes to influence. Not only because you're putting in the effort, it also gives you a front-row seat to be able to show empathy for others going through the same thing.

What I do know is that leaders who are part of the 23%ers live and breathe by their integrity. Are they making decisions and behaving in a way that is best for their people and their business, or are they looking for a quick fix?

The Five Principles of Influential Leadership

A true influential leader taps into the emotions of people and shows up in the best possible way. This ensures that the change they create has a lasting impact.

If you want to become this type of leader, think about these five principles of influential leadership.

1. Influence Is Built Upon A Foundation of Trust

A person who is not trusted has a limited ability to create and use influence.

One thing I always tell my team and clients is to do the right thing for the right reasons. When you don't just talk the talk but walk the walk, then you build trust.

People will rarely make a leap of faith for someone who hasn't earned their trust. On the other hand, most people will gladly take a blind step of faith for someone whom they have come to trust.

Studies show that customers will likely buy from trusted people rather than brands.

2. Influence Is Built Upon Making Others Successful

Back in my corporate days, this was my go-to strategy for influence. I loved to raise people up, make them super-skilled, so that they became successful (whatever their definition of success happened to be). This helped me out and also raised the trust within my team. As they became more successful and had lots of opportunities, I gained the reputation of a leader who created other leaders.

This principle is also referred to as the law of reciprocity. You're more likely to influence people by helping them achieve their goals. If you invest in making someone else successful then they in turn will likely be predisposed to helping you be successful.

Most people also refer to this as service leadership.

If you want to have a preview of how this works, watch the show *New Amsterdam*. The story centres around a public hospital with a new managing director who has some radical ideas to change things around. He comes in, asks "What can I do to help?" and removes blockers for his team. Ultimately you want your influence as a leader to be about removing blocker and or barries so that your people can do their best work and what you hired them to do.

A mistake I see brilliant leaders make is their own expectation to be the best at everything, rather than utilising the brilliance around them or hiring accordingly. It would be unreasonable for a leader to be the expert in all aspects of a team or department. Ideally, leaders are great at bringing out the best in people, enable teams to work cohesively together ,removing blockers, as ultimately making themselves redundant so that the team runs so well without them.

3. Influence Is Effective If You're Likeable

People do business with people they like. It's that simple.

If you want to influence people then you need to be approachable, positive, affable, trustworthy. You have to be a person of character and integrity.

No one wants to work with someone who is standoffish, pessimistic, and untrustworthy.

Of course, as human beings, there will be times when we feel empty, grumpy, or tired. When you're in this spot, have a think about how you can get back your likeability. If you need to take some time out, do it.

Self-care for leaders is important. You can't show up for your people and drive your business if you're not looking after yourself.

4. Influence Is Routed Through Helping Others Maintain Commitments

People respect professionals who keep their commitments. In the leadership world, people often judge you by your ability to keep your word and deliver your promises.

The key behind influencing via commitment lies in your ability to have people adopt an initial position that is consistent with a behaviour such that they are willing to agree to requests that are consistent with the prior commitment.

People desire to be perceived as dependable, reliable, and successful and will normally go to great lengths not to have their track record or their reputation tarnished.

Gaining strong commitments early on, and then simply holding people to their commitments, ultimately helps them enhance their reputation for delivering on promises made.

This is a two-pronged approach. As a role model, you keep your own commitments. As a leader of people, you enable your teams to keep their word and their commitment.

So, if there's something you need to sign off on, approve, or get out of the way for them, make sure you do that. This way, your people keep their commitments, and you don't create blockers along the way.

5. Influence Is Most Often Possessed By Those With Authority

As the popular saying goes: "With great power comes great responsibility." The same is true when you wear the people-leader hat. You have a huge responsibility to make sure you lead in a way that is congruent with yourself, the people around you, and the direction of the business.

It's also important to realise there is a reason for this statement:

"The highest authority is that which is given and rarely that which is taken."

The Trust Factor

Throughout your leadership journey being influential really comes down to one key thing. Do people trust you?

Steven Covey explored through the equation of trust.

Trust = Credibility + Reliability + Intimacy
Credibility—Do you know your stuff?
Reliability—Do you deliver what you say you're going to deliver?
Intimacy—How well do people know you, and how well are they connected to you?

Self-orientation—Do you care for your best interest? Or for others?

 (Credibility) Influence Is Most Often Possessed By Those With Authority.

Authority is most often given to those who display honesty, competency, expertise and wisdom. With authority comes credibility and with credibility comes influence.

Since those with the most authority will always have the most influence, it's important to remember to use your influence for the good of your people and your business.

Without the ability to influence others, you will find it hard to achieve traction for your people and business.

People now recognise the importance of influence leadership.

In the past, people could get away with being the "boss" and forcing people to follow top-down directions. In this new era of leadership, people don't necessarily have to listen or agree with you even if you're the leader.

If you want to learn how to incorporate these influence principles, then connect with me so we can work together to achieve this goal.

 ## (Reliability) Influence Is Routed Through Helping Others Maintain Commitments.

People respect professionals who keep their commitments. In the leadership world, people often judge you by your ability to keep your word and deliver your promises.

The key behind influencing via commitment lies in your ability to have people adopt an initial position that is consistent with behaviour such that they are willing to agree to requests that are consistent with the prior commitment.

People desire to be perceived as dependable, reliable and successful and will normally go to great lengths not to have their track record or their reputation tarnished.

Gaining strong commitments early on and then simply holding people to their commitments ultimately helps them enhance their reputation for delivering on promises made.

This is a two-pronged approach. As a role model, you keep your own commitments. As a leader of people, you enable your teams to keep their word and their commitment.

So if there's something you need to sign off on, approve or get out of the way for them, make sure you do that. This way, your people keep their commitments and you don't create blockers along the way.

 (Intimacy) Influence Is Most Effective When People Know Like And Trust You.

People do business with people they like. It's that simple.

If you want to influence people then you need to be approachable, positive, affable, trustworthy. You have to be a person of character and integrity.

No one wants to work with someone who is standoffish, pessimistic and untrustworthy.

Of course, as human beings, there will be times when we feel empty, grumpy or tired. When you're in this spot, have a think about how you can get back your likeability. If you need to take some time out, do it.

Self-care for leaders is important. You can't show up for your people and drive your business if you're not looking after yourself.

In the dance world this looked like gentle stretching, nourishing your body, yoga, and taking time away from theatres and lights.

In the corporate world this may look like time away from email, journaling, taking vacation time, and communicating your boundaries.

 (Self-Orientation) The Importance of Intention

It almost always come down to intent. What was their intent behind that comment or action?

Your intent as a leader is just as important as your influence. Clients who have worked with me know that my catch cry is *"all roads lead to the high road."* And that integrity really comes down to your intent as a leader.

Sue, my friend, colleague, and an exceptional woman in her own right, mentioned to me many years ago, *"Well, have you got your generous assumption goggles on?"* My generous assumption goggles, what are you on about? It's the lens in which you choose to perceive something; in this case it's the perception that people are trying their best, and most people want to get along within their workplace. What about you as a leader; what's your intent for yourself? Your team? Your impact?

I've included a few prompting questions below to help you figure out your intent.

Do You Want To Be A Good Leader Or A Great One?

In life, you can choose your own adventure, deciding what you can put in and removing what you don't need. It's the same as your leadership blueprint.

In this blog, we are going to tackle the leadership blueprint—how to create yours, and what it looks like.

Defining Your Expectations

One of the most common problems my clients face is conflict within their team and most of the time, it all comes down to expectations. Being really clear on what you expect from your team members and from yourself is so essential to working effectively.

Sometimes expectations are not met because they were not communicated early on. Aside from setting expectations at the very beginning, the expectations you create should be those that inspire and challenge you to be the best you can be. Make sure they are realistic and don't put strain on you and your team.

How can you set realistic expectations? By breaking your goals into chunks. It makes your goals more feasible to achieve and to sustain in the long run. Ask yourself and your team what tiny little thing can you do that will make you improve 1% more each day? This way you are lessening the overwhelm and building motivation and momentum.

What Will You Commit To As A Leader?

You don't have to know all the answers when creating your leadership blueprint, but having a commitment statement is a great way to set a clear path for yourself and your team. Finishing your blueprint with this statement shows commitment to everything written in your blueprint. You can also sign it to yourself (if that's your thing). Your commitment statement should show your dedication, intention, and focus to become the leader you want to be.

Do You Want To Be A Good Leader or A Great Leader?

Throughout history, great leaders have emerged with particular leadership qualities and styles. Understanding common leadership styles can help you define your own strengths and weaknesses to become a great leader. Here are the most common types of leadership:

Autocratic Leadership Style

Gone are the days of the autocratic leadership style (thank goodness!). The least liked but most common of what we think of as a leader is the autocratic leader. These people have high levels of control over their company and they make decisions on their own. This used to work back in the day, but in today's age, people want to be more involved and so, the autocratic leader won't always work well.

This type of leadership can work for people who are brand new and need constant supervision, or with smaller companies that have fewer employees, or during situations where there are quick decisions that need to be made. But this autocratic style shouldn't be used full time. It's more of a situational style of leadership.

Democratic Leadership Style

This leadership style values the inputs of the team. Democratic leadership is really good for making employees feel valued but it doesn't always work well for inexperienced teams or during situations that need quick decisions.

Servant Leadership

This leadership style is one where "you work for your team." It does seem noble; however, this type of leader gives too much to their teams to the point that they neglect their own needs. These leaders have been on a rise in previous years. While the idea is great, you are, however, useless if you are not taking care of yourself first.

Remember that self-care is never selfish. Fill your own cup first in order to show up as the best version of yourself for others.

By first knowing yourself and your type of leadership style, you get to find out what works best for your team. It is also an essential part of your leadership blueprint to clearly define your expectations and the commitment you are willing to make to your team and to yourself.

If you need more guidance with developing your own leadership blueprint you can find additional resources here: www.gruntgritandgrace.com.au

LESSON 7:

Leadership extends beyond a mere title; it's an inside-out job, requiring self-leadership before leading others. Influence, defined as the ability to affect the actions and decisions of others, is a key aspect of successful leadership, enabling leaders to achieve desired outcomes and make a lasting impact.

True influence comes from trust, commitment, and empathy. Leaders are urged to assess their own leadership styles, clarify expectations, and commit to a path that aligns with their values and goals.

I encourage you to invest in self-care and create a clear leadership blueprint, which outlines expectations, commitments, and the intention to lead with integrity. With these principles in mind, leaders can cultivate impactful influence and create a lasting positive effect on their teams and organisations.

Chapter 8

Luck and Leadership

★ ★ ★

"Optimists believe in good luck, pessimists in bad. But if it's all a matter of perspective, does luck even exist?"

Luck is often described as the meeting point between opportunity and preparedness. For many high-performing leaders, the idea of luck can seem like an elusive concept. They believe that their success is entirely based on hard work and determination, without considering the role that luck can play.

It's important to explore and understand the importance of luck in leadership and why it is essential for executives to have a new perspective on this often misunderstood concept. I challenge you to consider your perspective on luck, and how frequently you've brushed it off, or perhaps luck has been your go-to when things are going well.

There's a fascinating relationship between luck and leadership. Being aware of luck can shape your leadership path (or any path really), create unexpected opportunities, and transform your own leadership journey. I'd encourage you to embrace the idea of luck.

Luck isn't just about being in the right place at the right time. It is also about having the right perspective, having a positive mindset, being open to new ideas and possibilities, and embracing change. By shifting your mindset towards luck, you can see opportunities where others see obstacles.

This chapter is really about how you can cultivate a sense of luck in your daily life and how to create an environment that fosters luck in your team. There are some practical strategies that you can use to create your own luck and take advantage of opportunities when they arise.

Having a new perspective on luck can inspire high-performing leaders to take bold risks, embrace change, and seize opportunities that can transform their organisations.

Luck is not just a matter of chance, but it is a mindset that can be cultivated, and by adopting this mindset, executives can unlock their full potential and create new opportunities for themselves and their organisations.

Is It Luck, or Just Hard Work?

Growing up throughout my life, I heard the word *lucky* a lot. I've been told I was lucky. Luck, luck, lucky.

The funny thing about being lucky is that the more you believe it, the luckier you are.

There's research to suggest that one of the most interesting differentiators between lucky people and unlucky people is their attention on what opportunities are available to them and around them. And by all measures, I am a lucky person. I have a beautiful family, I live in a safe city, I have running water (and hot water). I am lucky, as are so many of you. But being told I was lucky really made me think and reflect on whether it was luck, or just hard work. Or perhaps a combination of both.

As a dancer in my teens, I was good enough to win competitions and perform the lead roles in performances and productions. However, that didn't just happen by luck (despite how frequently I was told so). That happened from the hundreds of thousands of hours I spent in the studio, rehearsing, falling down, getting back up, perfecting a step, and learning a routine until I could do it backwards, forwards, and inside out. This wasn't luck. It was sheer grunt, and wanting to do better, be better, and be at the top of my game, and The Game.

Grunt in the studio was doing a plié over and over again so that I could do it in my sleep, and sometimes it actually was in my sleep.

As a leader, luck and grunt might come disguised as you always having opportunities presented to you. *"Oh, you know Joe, everything just falls in his lap, he's so lucky." "Mary, yep, she's always in the right place at the right time, she's so lucky."* Is it luck though, or did Joe and Mary pay attention to the opportunities around them AND put in the work required to be in all the right places?

If you were inherently lucky, what would you wish for? What would you want to happen if it really were all down to luck?

Create Your Own Luck

In a 2018 study, science showed that luck is a self-fulfilling prophecy, according to Bloomsburg University professor Steven Hales, who conducted extensive research on luck and how people can increase their chances of being lucky. According to his research, there are several ways that leaders can create their own luck.

Firstly, leaders can increase their exposure to opportunities. This means putting themselves in situations where they are more likely to encounter lucky breaks. For example, attending networking events or conferences, or taking on new projects that stretch their skills and expose them to new people and ideas.

Secondly, leaders can develop a growth mindset. This means embracing challenges and viewing failures as learning opportunities rather than setbacks. By doing so, leaders can develop resilience and perseverance, which are essential traits for creating and capitalising on lucky opportunities.

Thirdly, leaders can cultivate a sense of curiosity and openness to new experiences. This means being receptive to different perspectives and actively seeking out new information and ideas. By doing so, leaders can expand their knowledge and increase their chances of encountering lucky opportunities.

Lastly, leaders can build strong relationships with others. This means investing time and energy in building and maintaining positive relationships with colleagues, mentors, and other people in their network. By doing so, leaders can create a supportive community that can help them identify and capitalise on lucky opportunities.

Overall, the key to creating your own luck as a leader is to be proactive, open-minded, and willing to take risks. By cultivating these traits and actively seeking out opportunities, leaders can increase their chances of experiencing lucky breaks and achieving their goals.

LESSON 8:

You'll find luck at the intersection of opportunity and preparedness.

There's an intriguing relationship between luck and leadership, challenging the notion that success is solely attributed to hard work and determination.

I want to emphasise that being proactive, positive, and willing to take calculated risks can empower you to create your own luck, unlock your full potential, and achieve your goals.

Chapter 9

Resilience and Repeatability

* ★ *

As a leader, the most important thing to consider when thinking about resilience is that it is not about avoiding failure or setbacks, but rather about learning to navigate them and emerge stronger from the experience.

This is a lesson that can be applied to both ballet and high performance in the corporate world.

In ballet, dancers must develop resilience to overcome physical challenges and setbacks, such as injuries or missed opportunities.

They must learn to push through pain and frustration in order to improve their technique and performance. This same resilience can be applied in the corporate world, where leaders must navigate challenges such as market disruptions, organisational changes, and unexpected setbacks.

One key to resilience is having a growth mindset, which means viewing challenges as opportunities for learning and growth rather than as obstacles to be avoided. This mindset allows leaders to stay focused on their goals and to persist in the face of setbacks.

Another important aspect of resilience is having a strong support system, both personally and professionally. This can include mentors, colleagues, and friends who can offer advice, guidance, and emotional support during challenging times.

Finally, leaders must take care of their physical and mental health in order to build resilience. This means getting enough sleep, exercise, and healthy food, as well as taking time for self-care and stress reduction activities such as meditation or yoga.

By taking care of themselves, leaders can better manage stress and bounce back from setbacks with greater ease and resilience.

Five Lessons Direct From the Ballet Studio on High Performance

1. Mental toughness: This involves the ability to stay focused, motivated, and confident even in the face of adversity. High-performing leaders can cultivate mental toughness by setting challenging goals, practising mindfulness, and engaging in positive self-talk.

2. Adaptability: Being able to adapt to changing circumstances and navigate uncertainty is crucial for high-performing leaders. They can build adaptability by being open to feedback, seeking out diverse perspectives, and staying curious and open-minded.

3. Self-care: High-performing leaders often neglect their own physical and emotional needs in the pursuit of their goals. Prioritising self-care, such as getting enough sleep, exercise, and nutrition, can help build resilience and prevent burnout.

4. Social support: Having a strong network of supportive colleagues, friends, and family can provide a buffer against stress and help high-performing leaders navigate difficult situations. Building and maintaining strong relationships can be an important aspect of resilience.

5. Learning from failures: High-performing leaders are not immune to failure, but they can use it as an opportunity for growth and learning. Embracing a growth mindset and reframing failures as learning

experiences can help build resilience and prevent setbacks from becoming insurmountable obstacles.

Ballet requires immense physical and mental resilience to endure the rigours of training, rehearsals, and performances. Dancers must maintain a high level of focus, discipline, and perseverance, even in the face of setbacks or injuries. These same qualities are essential for high-performing executive leaders, who must navigate complex and ever-changing business environments.

In addition, the emphasis on teamwork in ballet can also provide valuable lessons for executive leaders. Just as dancers must work together to achieve a cohesive and harmonious performance, leaders must foster a culture of collaboration and communication within their organisations. The ability to adapt to new roles and work closely with others towards a common goal is critical for success in both ballet and leadership.

Overall, the principles of resilience, focus, discipline, teamwork, and adaptability that are so essential in ballet can be directly applied to the challenges faced by high-performing executive leaders. By embracing these lessons from the dance floor to the boardroom, leaders can cultivate the mindset and skills necessary for success in their roles.

You need to constantly show up. We've been conditioned to say yes and put others' needs before our own.

However, you can't pour from an empty cup.

You need to take care of your mind, your body, and your soul so you can give your best to your team, your family, your friends, and your work.

Putting yourself last—I don't know how else to say this …

Martyr = Shmartyr

It's normal for leaders to put themselves last; it is so easy to keep saying yes, sometimes at your own detriment. We take on too much and then don't have time or energy left for ourselves.

This makes it more imperative for us to schedule and follow a self-care regime. On my podcast—Made For More—I interviewed Madhavi Parker: CEO of Positive Minds Australia, and she talks about self-care being as conscious and commonplace at regular hygiene practices.

Multifaceted Intentional Self-Care

Many people don't go for self-care guilt-free because they associate it with a trip to the gym, doing yoga, or having a day at the spa. Things that require a lot of time and effort to complete.

Rosie Bartlett, founder of Mindseye Training, says that self-care is more than those things. It has many aspects and layers such as:

- Physical—exercise or a walk on the beach
- Spiritual—meditation, religion, or just some alone time
- Connections—taking time to phone a friend or talk to your family
- Learning—reading for example

As you can see, self-care doesn't need to be expensive or strenuous. It also shouldn't be just one thing. It must be several actions that help you recharge your batteries.

Rosie recommends that you think of the dimensions you could potentially boost so you have a more holistic self-care regime. It's also important to schedule it; otherwise, it will never happen. You will either forget to do it or you will find excuses not to do it.

The intention behind the decision to do something for you and what it does for you matters.

Going for a walk to recharge versus just wandering about will give you different results. The former prepares your mind to achieve a goal of feeling better.

Zoning out is good. But will watching Netflix or scrolling on your phone for two hours leave you revived, refreshed, and ready to go? Will a glass of wine give the same results? If it does, then good for you. But is it your only form of self-care?

Remember, self-care needs to be holistic and involve different facets of your entire being.

Defining Boundaries For Self-Care

Having boundaries is important in self-care. You can't have people constantly intruding in on your "me" time. As noted above, you can't take care of yourself if you keep saying yes to others.

Setting boundaries means learning to say no, not just in your professional life but in your personal life as well. This may lead to some discomfort both for you and your team or your loved ones.

If you want help to transition towards setting healthy boundaries. Head to www.gruntgritandgrace.com for additional resources.

Self-Care Ritual

SPARE 5 MINUTES?
- TAKE A FEW DEEP BREATHS AND PRACTICE YOUR BOX BREATHING
- STRETCH YOUR BODY
- LISTEN TO YOUR FAVOURITE SONG

SPARE 15 MINUTES?
- MEDITATE FOR CLARITY/CALMNESS OR INTENTION SETTING
- READ A CHAPTER OF A BOOK
- JOURNAL OUT YOUR THOUGHTS

SPARE 30 MINUTES?
- TAKE A WALK OUTSIDE
- GET CRAFTY
- COOK A NEW RECIPE

SPARE 60 MINUTES?
- CATCH UP WITH A FRIEND
- READ A BOOK
- ATTEND A YOGA CLASS

The Seesaw Effect

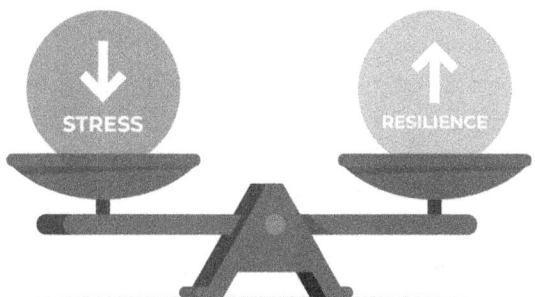

Resilience is one of the most important qualities that a leader can have. It allows leaders to navigate the challenges and setbacks that are inevitable in any complex undertaking. However, resilience is not a quality that can be developed overnight. It requires practice and repetition, just like any other skill. In this chapter, we will explore the importance of repeatable resilience activities and how they can help leaders avoid burnout and stress.

Resilience is defined as the ability to bounce back from setbacks, to adapt to change, and to maintain focus in the face of challenges. It is a critical skill for leaders because it allows them to navigate the uncertainties and complexities of the modern business world. However, resilience is not something that can be developed through a one-time effort. Instead, it requires consistent practice and repetition.

One of the keys to developing resilience is to create a routine of resilience activities that are repeatable. These activities should be easy to do, take little time, and be enjoyable. They should also be designed to help the leader recharge and recover from stress.

There are many different resilience activities that can be repeated, but some of the most effective include exercise, meditation, journaling, and spending time in nature. Exercise is particularly effective because it releases endorphins, which are natural mood boosters. Meditation is also useful because it helps to calm the mind and reduce stress. Journaling is helpful because it allows the leader to reflect on their thoughts and emotions, which can help them gain perspective and clarity. Spending time in nature is beneficial because it allows the leader to disconnect from technology and reconnect with the natural world.

It is important to note that resilience activities should be enjoyable and not feel like a chore. If an activity feels like a burden, it will not be sustainable in the long term. Leaders can experiment with different activities until they find the ones that work best for them.

Repeatable resilience activities are also important because they help to prevent burnout. Burnout is a state of physical, emotional, and mental exhaustion that can occur when a person is under constant stress for an extended period of time. Burnout is a common problem for high-performing leaders who work long hours and have demanding schedules.

By incorporating repeatable resilience activities into their daily routine, leaders can prevent burnout and maintain their energy and focus over the long term. They can also reduce their risk of developing chronic stress-related health problems.

Performance Training Is Actually Resilience Training

Performance training and resilience training are closely related because developing resilience is crucial for performing well under pressure and overcoming obstacles. Resilience training involves building skills and strategies that help individuals manage stress, recover from setbacks, and maintain a positive outlook in the face of challenges. This kind of training can be applied to a wide range of contexts, including sports, the performing arts, and leadership.

In ballet, dancers must constantly push themselves to improve their technique and perform at their best, despite the physical and mental demands of their craft. To do this, they must develop resilience by building strength, flexibility, and endurance, and by learning to manage their emotions and cope with the stress of performing. These skills are essential for achieving success in the highly competitive world of ballet.

Similarly, in leadership, resilience is critical for navigating the challenges of leading a team or organisation. Leaders must be able to manage their emotions, adapt to changing circumstances, and bounce back from setbacks in order to inspire and motivate their team members. They must also be able to stay focused on their goals and maintain a positive outlook, even in the face of adversity.

By connecting the dots between ballet and leadership, we can see that the skills and strategies used to develop resilience in one context can be applied to another. For example, leaders can learn from dancers how to manage stress and maintain focus under pressure, while dancers can learn from leaders how to inspire and motivate others. By taking a holistic approach to performance training and resilience training, we can develop the skills and strategies needed to succeed in any context.

Decision Fatigue and Simplification

In the fast-paced world of leadership and innovation, decision-making is a constant demand. As leaders, we are often confronted with countless choices every day, and form crucial business strategies to seemingly mundane tasks. However, the weight of these decisions can gradually wear down our mental energy, leading to a phenomenon known as decision fatigue.

I wanted to explore the concept of decision fatigue and draw inspiration from CEO and co-founder of Apple Inc., Steve Jobs, who is said to have employed a simple yet powerful strategy to combat this challenge. By understanding the importance of reducing decision fatigue, you can optimise your leadership effectiveness and drive greater success in your organisation.

Understanding Decision Fatigue

Decision fatigue is the mental exhaustion that arises from making numerous choices throughout the day. As leaders, we constantly face a barrage of decisions, both big and small, and this can overwhelm our cognitive resources. When your mental energy is depleted, your ability to make well-informed and rational decisions diminishes, leading to potential mistakes, and in my own experience, a shorter fuse.

Steve Jobs, the visionary leader behind Apple's success, recognised the detrimental impact of decision fatigue on his leadership prowess. To maintain a clear and focused mind, he adopted a unique practice— wearing the same outfit every day. This seemingly simple decision had a profound impact on his ability to lead effectively.

- Simplification: By adopting a consistent wardrobe, Jobs eliminated the daily task of *choosing* what to wear. This act of simplification allowed him to redirect his mental energy towards more critical aspects of his role, such as product innovation and strategic planning.

- Enhanced Focus: With reduced decision fatigue, Jobs' ability to concentrate and think creatively improved significantly. He could immerse himself fully in the visionary projects without being bogged down by trivial choices.

Practical Application

While adopting a uniform wardrobe might not be the right fit for every leader (myself included!) there are valuable lessons we can draw form Steve Jobs' approach to reduce day-to-day decision fatigue.

1. Prioritise critical decisions: Identify the most important decisions you need to make each day and allocate sufficient time and focus to address them effectively. Delegate less critical choices to streamline your decision-making process.

2. Create routine and rituals: Establishing daily routines and rituals can help reduce the number of decisions you need to make, allowing you to concentrate on high-priority tasks with a clear mind.

3. Embrace simplicity: Seek opportunities to simplify processes, communication, and systems within your organisation. Eliminating

unnecessary complexities can enhance overall efficiency and minimise decision fatigue.

4. Take breaks and practise self-care: Regular breaks and self-care activities, such as mindfulness exercises, physical activity, or spending time in nature, can help rejuvenate your mental energy and combat decision fatigue.

As leaders, we must acknowledge the significant impact of decision fatigue on our decision-making abilities and overall leadership effectiveness. By adopting strategies to reduce decision fatigue, inspired by the simplicity of Steve Jobs' approach, we can maintain focus, enhance creativity, and lead with clarity and purpose.

Remember, it's not about replicating Steve Jobs' wardrobe; it's about recognising the value of simplification and streamlining decisions to become better leaders in an increasingly complex world. Embrace the power of decision fatigue reduction, and you'll find yourself better equipped to drive success in your organisation and inspire your teams to achieve greatness.

LESSON 9:

How we do one thing, is how we do all things.

Creating your own operating system for what feels right and what gets the results you're after is the key to being able to repeat that action, behaviour and result. In this day and age where we're more busy than ever before, it's important to recognise that sometimes we have to slow down to speed up, whether that's active recovery after a solid performance season, or additional self care in readiness for a stressful period.

Being aware of what you need to do your best is key to getting what you want.

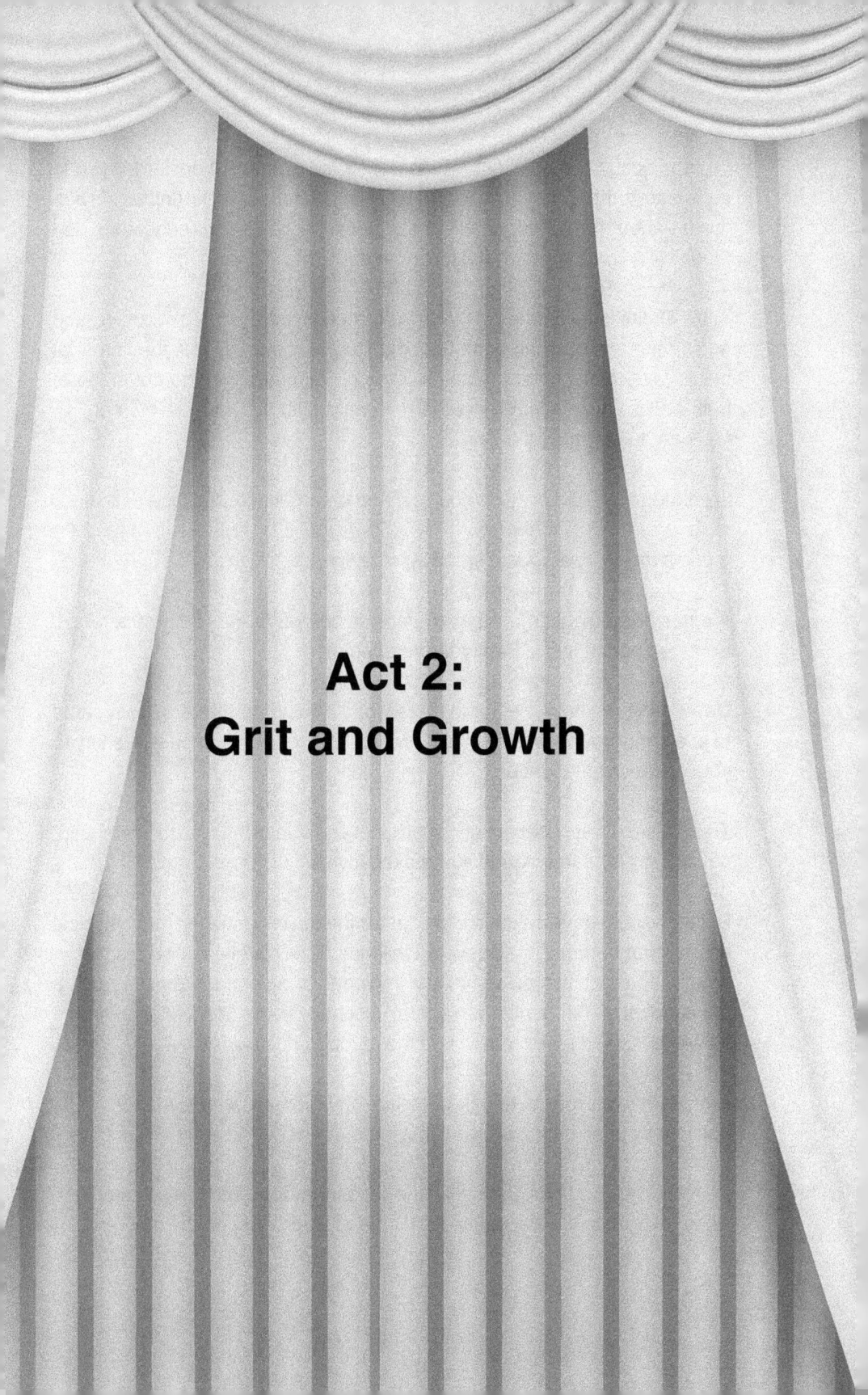

Act 2:
Grit and Growth

I was looking for a succinct way to define grit to make it easier for you to understand the concept … but I think my perspective is unique. We're talking about the interconnectedness between ballet and leadership, so I thought I'd share my own definition here.

Ally's Definition—Grit is a little bit like a rehearsal. You do it again, and again, and again; it can be boring, monotonous even. Grit is the fibre that builds growth, both the mental and the physical. During the grit stage of both ballet and leadership you are literally teaching muscle memory so you can do it without thinking.

Cambridge definition—Grit: courage and determination despite difficulty:

It takes true (= real) grit to stand up to a bully.

It's not hard. You've just never done it before to know the difference. Engage your curiosity. Shift your perspective.

Developing grit is crucial for leaders who are high performers. Being able to push past your own limits, and overcoming your limiting beliefs is key to your success as a leader.

This concept is applicable not just to ballet and dance but also to leadership, particularly for senior leaders and executives.

Ballet dancers have an unyielding determination to push past their physical and mental barriers to achieve excellence. The countless hours spent in practice, perfecting their technique, and performing under pressure require a great deal of grit. Similarly, leaders must have the resilience to overcome challenges, lead by example, and make tough decisions.

Any leadership role is a high-pressure environment where leaders must continually push past their own limits and limitations to achieve success.

Developing grit means embracing the challenges that come with leadership, working through the discomfort, and emerging stronger on the other side. It means committing to a growth mindset and staying dedicated to personal and professional development, even when faced with adversity.

Leaders can learn valuable lessons from ballet and the performing arts, particularly in the areas of focus, discipline, and perseverance. Just as a dancer must focus on perfecting their technique and performance, a leader must focus on achieving their goals and driving the success of their team or organisation.

Chapter 10

The Virtues of Grit

When writing this chapter, I spent a long time researching and ruminating on what grit actually is. Much like the grittiness of sand, I feel that grit is a tactile virtue, it's a feeling. Throughout my research, it was clear that virtues of grit all share a common thread of a strong commitment to achieving one's goals and overcoming obstacles along the way.

The Three Ps of Grit

Virtues of Grit

Purpose
In leadership, in the corporate world, we often talk about our purpose or our mission or why it is we do the things that we do.

"My mission is to change the way we lead and talk at work, so that everyone can go home to their families at the end of the day, and enjoy the company that's around the table rather than having to decompress and destress from a toxic workplace, leader or team."
Ally Nitschke

I think when it comes to grit, one of the virtues of grit is having faith. Faith that you are on the right track, faith that things are all going to work out in the end, faith that you can hold on for that little bit longer, to be able to do the hard thing. Grit is really around the belief in yourself, belief in your abilities, faith in yourself, faith that there is something much bigger than you that is going to keep you on track. And I think to practise your faith it really does involve a level of surrender to let things happen. Surrender is a hard lesson to learn but something that we need to grab on to, hold on to, in order to embody that virtue of Grit.

Persistence

Perseverance, tenacity, and determination are all related to the quality of persistence, but they have slightly different nuances.

Perseverance

Perseverance refers to the ability to continue working towards a goal despite obstacles, setbacks, or difficulties. It involves a steadfastness of purpose and a commitment to seeing things through to the end, even when the going gets tough.

Perseverance is perhaps the most important lesson that ballet can teach us about leadership. The countless hours of practice and repetition required to perfect a dance performance require a great deal of perseverance. In the same way leaders must persevere in the face of adversity, setbacks, and obstacles. Perseverance is what allows us to push past our own limitations and achieve success.

Perseverance means being hardworking and finishing what is started, despite barriers and obstacles that arise.

I like to think of it as white-knuckling. As my coach would say, "You're just on the wrong side of a lot of hard work!"

The pleasure received from completing what you're setting out to achieve is very important to those who value perseverance, usually people who are high performers and high achievers.

Conviction Is The Secret Sauce Between Persistence And Perseverance.

When you know, then you know that you know.

Leaders are often responsible for implementing change, guiding the team, generating enthusiasm within the team, solving a problem, or seizing an opportunity. All of these actions require one important trait: conviction.

Can a person be a leader without conviction? It is possible, but they can't be a great leader who motivates and inspires others to change and improve.

Conviction means showing actual passion about your beliefs and values

Conviction sparks passion, which is a great energizer for the whole team, because passion and energy are infectious to those around you.

It is showing actual passion about your beliefs and your values while demonstrating consistent behaviour. Leaders with conviction have an unwavering belief in their ability to control things that they can and analyse facts for what they are.

But if conviction in a leader is so valuable, why is it an increasingly rare trait?

Not being able to show conviction as a leader stems from not being clear with your leadership brand and not having the confidence in what you know and finding out what you don't know. This all stems from Clarity and Confidence which I discuss in detail in my first book Rise of the Courageous Leader.

Uncertainty takes up a lot of our mental energy. So having conviction makes us more effective in our job as a leader. When you make fast and rapid decisions that are aligned with your values, you are able to practise that conviction muscle and produce better results.

When leaders have conviction, they are strong without being harsh. To be a more influential leader, practise your conviction muscle by starting with small decisions first, then working up to the bigger ones.

When Purpose And Persistence Collide = Tenacity

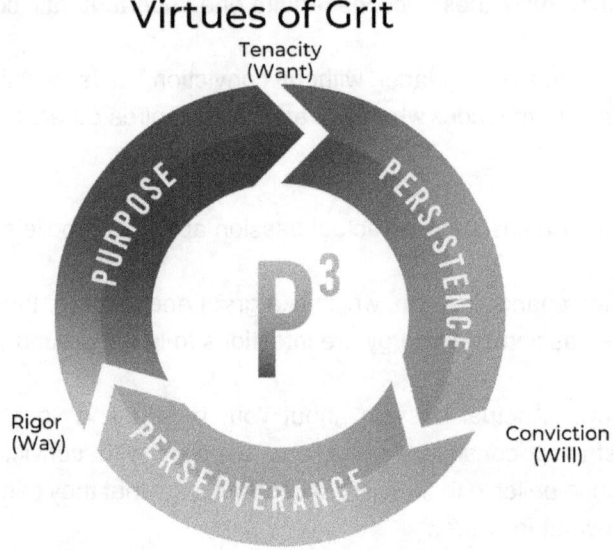

I'm lucky enough to work with some exceptional leaders. And the one thing they all have in common is that they haven't stopped learning, growing, developing, or asking for help. This is tenacity, and it's a vital capability of courageous leaders and 23%ers.

Tenacity implies a dogged determination to keep going in the face of adversity. It suggests an unyielding resolve and an unwillingness to give up or back down, no matter how difficult the challenge.

Tenacity means continually striving for what's next. It means seeking out a greater level of connection and working towards creating a larger impact. It means committing to this leadership gig, and giving it all you've got with determination, resilience, grit, and persistence.

Tenacity is a vital capability of leaders. In fact, it's described by Nancy Eberhardt, executive coach and CEO of Pathwise Partners in *Forbes*, as the

"single greatest factor for success which can take a team from doing all right to thriving."

This is the ability to persevere despite challenges and to learn from mistakes so you can try again. So it doesn't mean not failing. Instead, it means failing and trying again until you finally do succeed.

Today's world is often about quick fixes and immediate ROIs. So when things get challenging, or messy, or you're met with failure, too often people walk away. Great, courageous leaders embrace those challenges, communicating with authenticity and candour and finding solutions with long-term focus and methodologies. And that's tenacity.

Rigour = The Love Child Of Purpose And Perseverance

Rigour refers to the quality of being extremely thorough, accurate, and precise in your work or actions. It involves a strong attention to details, a commitment to excellence, and a willingness to work hard to achieve your goals. The quality of rigour involves a strong work ethic and a willingness to put in the effort necessary to succeed. The effort necessary to become a 23%er.

Rigour is a quality that is valued in both the ballet world and in leadership. In ballet, rigour refers to the discipline and attention to detail required in the execution of technique and performance. It is essential for a ballet dancer to have rigour in order to achieve mastery and excellence in their art.

Similarly, in the world of leadership, rigour refers to the ability to be methodical, systematic, and precise in one's approach to problem-solving and decision-making. It involves an attention to detail and a commitment to thoroughness that enables leaders to make well-informed and effective decisions.

Having rigour is important for leaders who aspire to reach a c-suite position. C-suite positions, such as CEO, CFO, and COO, require individuals to have a strong sense of rigour in their leadership style. These positions often involve overseeing complex and challenging operations, and the ability to approach these tasks with discipline and precision is essential.

Leaders who demonstrate rigour in their work are often seen as reliable and effective, which can help them to build credibility and trust with their colleagues and superiors. This, in turn, can increase their chances of being considered for c-suite positions, where a rigorous approach is typically required.

Perseverance emphasises endurance, tenacity emphasises persistence, and determination emphasises focused resolve. However, all three of these qualities share a common thread of persistence and a refusal to give up in the face of adversity.

Knowing Self

I think grit really is the showing of someone's character, what kind of person they are. What kind of person are you? In my first book, *Rise of the Courageous Leader*, the first pillar we talk about is self-aware; this is true for grit too. What are you really made of?

As a child, we had a lot of books in our house, and a collection of tiny books, very small-sized books. There was one that I'd climb with into my parents'

bed each Sunday morning to read. It was a book about the type of person you were, your character, based on which day of the week you were born.

I don't remember the title of the nursery rhyme book, but I do remember the words.

Monday's child is fair of face,
Tuesday's child is full of grace
Wednesday's child is full of woe,
Thursday's child has far to go,
Friday's child is loving and giving
Saturday's child works had for his living
And the child that is born on the
Sabbath day is bonny
and blithe and good and gay.

Now, I don't know how true this is, but I used to read it over and over again as a young girl to try to understand who I was, and who I was meant to be.

Was I destined to be a particular person because of the day of the week I was born? What if I was born in another country, which meant "technically" I was born on another day. Ahhh, so many questions, from such a young age.

From our early childhood year, we're conditioned to conform to societal expectation, not rock the boat. As a woman and a young girl, there's conditioning to be a carer, and make sure everyone's needs are met. I think while the intention for this in childhood was good, the impact it has in adult hood has left many people having to unlearn some of their identity beliefs.

You know those times when you don't really know how to fit in. I think for many people, particularly high achievers, they're looking at why they don't quite fit in, and continually seeking answers that make sense.

My first foray into professional development was in 2005. I remember it as clear as day. There was an internal memo that went out asking for submissions to a professional development workshop titled Pac(wo)

men with the bracket. The facilitator was named Shivani Gupta. That day in 2005 unlocked my passion for further developing and learning with intention rather than just "plodding" through life.

Sure, there are plenty of tools we can use to fast-track the knowing of self, and I'd highly encourage you to continue that pursuit of really unpacking who you are and what you're about.

What's important to keep in mind when on a journey through grit and digging deep and looking for what it is that makes you YOU is that you get to choose.

You can choose and decide how you want to show up as a leader, you can choose how much you lean into courage, and more importantly, discomfort; that's when real courage is tested. You get to decide the pieces of intel you want to pick up and run with, and leave the bit behind that don't matter.

And here's the other thing. We all go through stages and seasons and journeys of leadership; it's okay to let something go that served you well, that's no longer a fit for you right now. Perhaps previously you were a people pleaser and now your circumstances have changed and you need to fiercely and kindly put in place some boundaries. Perhaps you're looking to make that next step to the exec team and your larrikin reputation no long reflects (or serves) the kind of leader that you are or want to be.

Change is okay, letting go is okay, turning over a new leaf, it's all okay. Change takes courage, and it's all a journey to getting to know yourself, and ultimately learning who you want to be.

The Unsexy Side of Grit

There's a side of grit that we don't really talk about. That's the unsexy side, the ugly crying, the sleepless nights, the stress, the doubt, the confusion and that feeling of being downright rudderless in the sea of life.

In the ballet world, what audiences see are the polished and pristine ballerinas in their tutu, with perfect buns and stage makeup. What audiences don't see is the grit that's been put in to get to the effortless piece.

Years ago I was the lead in the ballet *Cinderella*, it was my first major role, and I was so grateful and humbled to be given the role.

At some point in the final dress rehearsal I dipped into the finishing ponché (kind of like vertical splits) and my pointe shoe snapped. I rolled my ankle, and accidentally face-planted my teacher on the way down, which is very embarrassing when you're 15. I spent the night with my ankle elevated and an icepack on rotation.

The next morning, it was show day; it was the day where the theatre would be packed. There would be that buzz of excitement and I was ready; I'd put in the hard work, I'd put in the grunt. I'd rehearsed for hundreds of hours in studio after studio. The first performance was a matinee. And I was standing on the side of the stage in the wings waiting for the curtain to go up for the opening scene of Cinderella was sweeping the floors. And I was all of a sudden absolutely overcome with emotion to the point where I was bawling my eyes out on the side of the stage. And as they say, the show must go on. So I walked on crying with wild thoughts running through my mind.

Oh my goodness, what am I going to do? How will I ever do this? I'm not good enough. And I went through the steps which by then had become muscle memory. I left that first scene and walked off the side of the stage, really giving myself a good telling off for being "pathetic" and not being able to control my emotions.

Some of the crew who were in the audience came to congratulate me on what a realistic performance that was because, you know, in the scene, Cinderella was sweeping the floor and here I was walking onto the stage, bawling my eyes out. And it was in that moment that I knew that I had what it took to be able to do the work that I needed to do, but I tell you what, there's a side that's not seen; it's the blood, the sweat, the tears, the blisters, the falls, the strains, and the exhaustion. All of this goes on backstage (pun intended).

Earlier in Chapter 3 we talked about comparing your beginning with someone else's middle. The same applies to comparing your backstage story to the closing night performance. They're going to be poles apart.

LESSON 10:

Tenacity wins everyday of the week. It's often said it takes 10 years to become an overnight success, that success is directly related to consistency and tenacity over that period of time. Success is the result of relentless dedication, perseverance and practice throughout that journey.

Your success is the result of that work through your own leadership journey.

Chapter 11

Friction and Fire

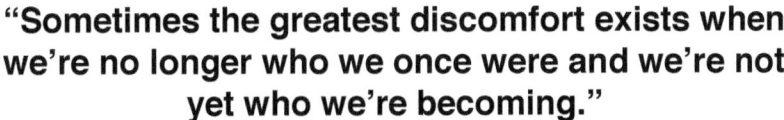

"Sometimes the greatest discomfort exists when we're no longer who we once were and we're not yet who we're becoming."

Grit is an essential characteristic that enables high achievers to persevere through tough times. It is the ability to hold on and persist when things get difficult. Grit requires passion, which is the fuel that keeps us going when faced with adversity. Leaders who possess grit understand that success is not just about speed but also about stamina, and they inspire their teams to develop a similar mindset.

Passion and grit go hand in hand, as grit is what builds stamina. It takes perseverance and determination to develop the physical, mental, and emotional stamina required to keep going when exhausted. The grit and perseverance required to be a successful leader or high achiever are akin to the gruelling and rigorous hours dancers spend practising, repeating the same moves again and again until they get it right.

One of the keys to developing grit is to win your own game, focusing on your own progress and growth rather than comparing yourself to others. It is essential to make small incremental improvements over time, as these add up to significant gains. As mentioned earlier in Chapter 3, the 1% improvement, sticking through the boredom, and the mental toughness where you feel you're not making progress is really setting you up with a strong foundation for the next stage, which is to be able to lead with grace.

Win Your Own Game

"In the race for success, speed is less important than stamina."
B.C Forbes, Founder of Forbes

Grit is the in-between bit that builds stamina. It's holding on when things get tough. If you're someone who lifts weights at the gym, it's that last set that burns, but you know next time it's going to be worth it.

As a dancer, grit was absolutely integral to being "game ready." The gruelling and rigorous hours spent practising over and over again can make or break even the most purpose-driven dancer.

There's a well-known joke in the ballet world that the teacher will often say:

"Let's see it one more time."

They're referring to an exercise or a routine … but what they really mean is, let's see it again and again and again. The joke is that never has a teacher said let's see it one more time, and only let's see it one.more.time. Building up the physical stamina as well as the mental and sometimes emotional stamina to keep going when you're exhausted takes grit, perseverance, and persistence.

In my mid-twenties, my best friend moved to Melbourne (from Adelaide) for a career opportunity and to live a little. I went to visit her often and one day while out and about shopping I came across a t-shirt that simply said "win your own game." I immediately bought that shirt. I love it. I wore it to every training session when learning how to run (I'll leave it up to you to decide whether I didn't train that often or did frequent loads of laundry). That t-shirt, the message that it meant to me, was that it didn't matter how fast I was at running, or even if I was any good. What mattered was what I thought about myself, and my own progress. It removed the need for comparisonitis. It made me feel invincible. It was my north star and reminder of what I was doing while I was training.

I think that's really what grit is about. It's about leaving behind the "*shoulds*," the *"coulds,"* the comparisons, the "*not enoughs*" and the continual cycle to benchmark yourself. Winning at your own game is simply that. Your Own Game.

Remove the Friction

Brendon Burchard, a high-performance expert, has looked at the data of over 250,000 high performers from around the world, from Olympians to fortune 500 top performers. He has found six key things high performers consistently do.

1. Seek clarity—What's the vision of their future?
2. Generate energy—What do they do to build their energy and vitality?
3. Raise necessity—Making sure the work they're doing is important.
4. Increase productivity—Focusing on what's going to move the needle.
5. Develop influence—Developing their leadership brand.
6. Demonstrate courage—Pushing themselves outside of their comfort zone.

One of my favourite techniques he talks about in Generate Energy is Remove Friction.

Sometimes it's not necessarily that you need to do something better, sometimes it's something that is causing you friction that you could improve to maximise time and energy.

To give you an example, I have four children under the age of eight, all boys (yes, it's crazy!). If you have small children you'll understand when I say four children somehow equates to laundry maths as having 1100 pairs of socks, and shoes.

For a long while, every morning we'd go through what I (lovingly) called "sock gate." Without fail, it would be a 45-minute exercise for each of the kids to go upstairs, find their socks from their respective drawers, come back down the stairs, and find a matching pair of shoes. Put said shoes and socks on and get into the car. Every day, 45 minutes, of having "the wrong socks," sometimes forgetting to put both on, missing a shoe (how one can take one shoe off downstairs and the other off upstairs is lost on me). Every morning this went on; as you can imagine, there was some yelling and frustration for everyone involved.

When I read Brendon Burchard's book, *High-Performance Habits*, I was immediately drawn to the friction section. Instantly I knew we had to make some changes to the "sock gate" that was causing so much friction.

Instead, we (my husband and I) looked at how we could make it easy for everyone. Now we have a communal kids' sock basket; during laundry time ALL socks get put into the same basket. Each morning there's no searching for socks. Everyone has the same colour socks, making pairing the socks a breeze, and what was a 45-minute activity that caused quite a bit of stress is now a 10-minute exercise and (mostly) a smooth-sailing morning. Not only is there a lot less stress we now also have an extra 30 minutes in the morning and start the day off better rather than everyone yelling and screaming at each other.

What's a "sock gate" equivalent you could implement? What's causing you friction that you could remove?

Pushing Limits

Grit—striving for excellence and brilliance. Grit is the determination and perseverance to push your own limits.

"Success is a few simple disciplines, practiced every day, while failure is simply a few errors in judgement, repeated every day."
Jim Rohn

Grit is the unyielding determination to push past our own limits and achieve excellence. It encompasses the physical, emotional, and belief-based limitations that we place on ourselves, and requires a level of discipline, focus, and perseverance that is not always easy to achieve.

The concept of grit is closely tied to the idea of pushing our limits, both physically and mentally. It means pushing through the discomfort, the pain, and the doubts that arise when we attempt to achieve something beyond what we have accomplished before. It requires the courage to step outside of our comfort zones and embrace the challenges that come with growth and development.

Physical limits are often the most visible and tangible, but emotional and belief-based limits can be just as difficult to overcome. Emotional limits may arise when we encounter setbacks or failures and begin to doubt our own abilities or worth. Belief-based limits may arise from societal norms or expectations, or from our own internalised messages about what we are capable of achieving.

Grit requires us to push past all of these limits, to strive for excellence and brilliance in everything we do. It means committing to a growth mindset, and embracing the challenges that come with it.

Jim Rohn's quote highlights the importance of discipline in achieving success. Success is not the result of one big decision or one major accomplishment, but rather the culmination of small disciplines and practices that we engage in every day. Failure, on the other hand, often arises from repeated errors in judgement, a lack of discipline or consistency, or a failure to push past our own limitations.

To develop grit, we must cultivate discipline, consistency, and perseverance in our daily lives. This means setting goals, creating routines, and committing to a plan of action. It means staying focused on the long-term vision, even when faced with setbacks or obstacles.

We can also cultivate grit by embracing discomfort and challenge in our daily lives. This might mean taking on new challenges, pursuing new interests or hobbies, or engaging in activities that push us outside of our comfort zones. It means learning to embrace failure as an opportunity for growth, rather than as a reflection of our worth or abilities.

Ballet dancers are a prime example of individuals who embody grit in all its forms. They must push past their physical limitations, engaging in hours of practice and training to perfect their technique and performance. They must also push past emotional and belief-based limitations, staying focused and committed even in the face of rejection or criticism.

The lessons of grit that we learn from ballet and other disciplines can be applied to all aspects of our lives, including our personal and professional goals. Whether we are striving to achieve success in our careers, our relationships, or our personal growth, grit is a critical component of that journey.

Grit is the unyielding determination to push past our own limits and achieve excellence. It requires a level of discipline, consistency, and perseverance that is not always easy to achieve, but is critical to achieving success in all aspects of our lives. By cultivating grit through daily disciplines and embracing discomfort and challenge, we can push past our physical, emotional, and belief-based limitations, and strive for excellence and brilliance in all that we do.

LESSON 11:

So often we spend time (and energy) trying to jam more into our days and our lives rather than looking to remove what's causing us to need more time in our days and lives.

Get rid of the thing/s that are causing you friction.... Especially if it's your own mindset that getting in the way of your brilliance.

Chapter 12

Patience and Persistence

★ ⭐ ★

"Good things take time."
My Dad

Growing up on the farm, I was always so impatient, impatient for the lambs to arrive (they were very cute), impatient for the rain to stop so that I could play, and impatient for my siblings to grow up a little bit more. In the studio, I was impatient to get started, I was impatient to see success and improvement. They say patience is a virtue. I used to frequently joke that patience was a virtue I didn't care to possess until someone reframed it for me to:

"Patience really is our ability to tolerate the passing of time."

Both learning a ballet move and growing as a leader requires patience and persistence for different reasons.

In the case of learning a ballet move, it takes time and practice to develop the necessary muscle memory and technique to execute the move properly. This process can be frustrating and may involve setbacks and failures along the way. Patience is necessary to persevere through these challenges and continue to work towards mastery of the move. Additionally, persistence is needed to continue practising the move regularly, even when progress may seem slow or non-existent.

Similarly, growing as a leader also requires patience and persistence. Becoming an effective leader involves developing a wide range of skills, from communication and decision-making to problem-solving and conflict resolution. It takes time and experience to hone the skills and develop the necessary confidence and competence to lead effectively.

Patience is required to stay focused on the long-term goal of becoming a better leader, even when progress may seem slow or when facing setbacks. Persistence is needed to continue developing these skills through consistent effort and ongoing learning, even in the face of challenges or failures.

Consistency Compounds

"Most people overestimate what they can do in 12 months, and underestimate what they can achieve in five years."

There is a saying in the ballet world that you learn fifth to forget it. For context, fifth position is the position of the feet where they're crossed over heel to toe. It's also typically the first position people try when they're pretending to do a ballet move. Imagine your feet turned inside out. That's the position.

In ballet when you learn fifth to forget it means you practise it so much, it's almost every starting position that eventually you'll be standing in fifth without even thinking about it. The muscle memory is so ingrained that you don't need to think about it, you don't need to try, your feet just find the position.

This is the grit part. Doing the same thing over and over again until it's so ingrained that you don't even notice, and things happen without effort or attention.

Blind Belief

In the high stakes world of leadership, navigating and embarking on a journey can sometimes feel like a map that's yet to be drawn. Setting your own path, leaning into your own belief requires profound trust in your vision, your strategy and you ability to adapt and navigate unforeseen obstacles along the way.

Many of my clients who cultivate this mindset understand that the landscape is forever changing and evolving. More recently this can elude predictions and defy expectation. In our current environment, blind belief becomes that catalyst for action, enabling leaders to take the first step, even when they can't anticipate the outcome.

They key to success lies in the symbolic relationship between blind belief and calculated risk-taking. While leaders must rely on data and analysis to inform many decisions, there comes a juncture where you have the option to jeté into the unknown.

Blind belief is the driving force that propels you forward when logic along cannot provide a definitive path. It is the audacity to experiment, innovate and challenge the status quo, all while understanding that not every step will be illuminated by certainty.

In a corporate setting, where the pursuit for excellence is relentless, embracing blind belief is not a gamble, it's a calculated endeavour rooted in the understanding that progress often emerges from the shadows of the unknown. Inspired leaders, lead by example, encourage their teams to trust in the vision, to persevere when results are elusive, and to forge new pathways towards corporate success.

Blind belief when harnessed effectively, is the compass to navigate uncharted waters, guiding you towards unparalleled achievements and unanticipated triumphs.

LESSON 12

Illuminate your own path...

In the journey of self-discovery, it's essential to embrace the wisdom and the path that often appears elusive. It's like a lotus that emerges from the depths of muddy water or the diamond that forms under immense pressure. These transformative moments occur when we let the cracks in our understanding allow the light to penetrate.

Trusting this process can be challenging because it requires us to have faith in a sense of direction that might not make sense, just like a plane turns into the wind to take off. It's about believing that every obstacle and detour is a necessary part of our growth, even when it seems like we're moving backwards (or not moving at all). It's the understanding that in the grand design of our personal evolution, there's purpose in every twist and turn.

With each step you illuminate your own path, you move closer to trusting your true self and allowing the light of wisdom and self-discovery shine through the cracks of your understanding.

Chapter 13

Mistakes and Mis-steps

★ ★ ★

Throughout my childhood, my family and I spent every summer holiday camping at a caravan park. These are some of my favourite memories; we started going when I was eight, and there's still a tent set up every January to this day.

One warm summer evening as a young teen I remember sitting in my dome tent in front of my CD player and madly pausing and playing a song that I really wanted the lyrics to. The song was "Everybody's free (to wear sunscreen)"—it's a banger. Great lyrics. I've included them in the back of the book for your own reference. There's one particular line that really stuck with me: "Make mistakes."

If you've been a teenager or you have teenagers, there are a lot of mistakes to be made. The key learning here is, what did you learn from them, and what can you learn from them?

While you're in the grit phase of leadership, it's absolutely okay, expected, and quite important to make mistakes. Mistakes can be messy progress; the key thing here is around progress. Unless you're a brain surgeon and precision is key (this is not the book for you), there's very little that can't be fixed or mended.

We learn from mistakes.

Own Your Mistakes

One of the most gracious things a leader can do is own their mistakes and then learn from them.

In Chapter 10, "The Virtues of Grit," we discussed the importance of persistence. When it comes to reframing failure, this is the mindset on what failure and ultimately what mistakes actually mean. When we think making a mistake means failure, we're reluctant to make mistakes in case we fail. What if, instead of mistakes, you actually were going through a different process of learning.

It's okay to make mistakes; just turn around, fix them up, and recognise what you've learned.

But ultimately, the hard work that you're putting in now is for the future.

Thermostat vs Thermometer

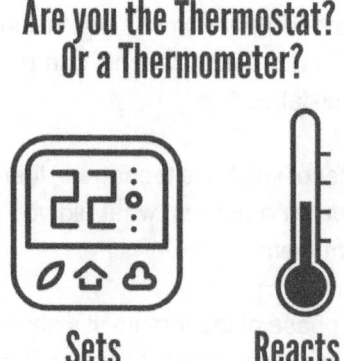

One of the hardest steps in ballet to master is the fouetté, most famously in the ballet *Swan Lake* where the white swan sticks her leg out to the front and swings it to the side to turn in a pirouette (circle). The coordination, speed, precision, plus making sure not to get dizzy makes this step a very tricky one to master, yet with the right training and muscle memory, it can be achieved. What happens when people begin to learn this step is their mindset gets in the way. Instead of simply letting their body do what it's been training to do, they give in to the fear and they react to that fear.

With the leaders that I work with often we talk about whether they're the thermostat or the thermometer. Do they walk into a room and react to what's going on in there as a thermometer reacts to a changing environment? Or do they walk into the room and set the temperature, much like a thermostat? In this example, setting the temperature of the room is akin to setting the tone, the expectations, the social norms. Seasoned leaders will know, particularly those who have been through a crisis, how a leader responds in a crisis will deeply impact the team around them.

Thomas Edison said when asked about his failures inventing the lightbulb.

"I didn't fail, I found 10,000 ways it didn't work."

If you've feared failure in the past and it's kept you stuck, the best time to start is right now. Give yourself some grace as a leader. Mistakes happen—balls get dropped, you can find them exactly where you left them. Pick those balls up, take a deep breath, and carry on with determination.

Grow Through Your Mistakes

The fear of failure can be paralysing. Many of us are so afraid of making mistakes that we avoid taking risks or trying new things altogether. But as Carol Dweck points out in her book, *Mindset: The New Psychology of Success*, the most successful people are those who embrace a growth mindset, viewing mistakes as opportunities for learning and growth rather than as indicators of failure.

In ballet, mistakes are an integral part of the learning process. No dancer becomes perfect overnight, and even the most accomplished professionals make mistakes in rehearsals and performances. But it's through those mistakes that dancers learn what works and what doesn't, refine their technique, and grow as performers.

The same is true in leadership. No leader is infallible, and mistakes are an inevitable part of the job. But it's how leaders respond to those mistakes that sets them apart. A leader who embraces a growth mindset is willing to admit when they've made a mistake, learn from it, and use that knowledge to make better decisions in the future.

Failure can be a powerful teacher. When we fail, we learn what doesn't work and what we need to do differently. Failure can also help us develop resilience and grit, two qualities that are essential for success in any field.

But the key is to view failure not as a reflection of our worth or competence, but as an opportunity for growth. As Dweck notes, "We can choose to believe that our abilities are fixed and finite, or we can choose to believe that we can always improve and grow." The latter mindset is what allows us to embrace our mistakes and use them to become better versions of ourselves.

Of course, this doesn't mean that we should actively seek out failure. Rather, we should be willing to take risks and try new things, knowing that failure is always a possibility. And when we do fail, we can approach the situation with curiosity and a willingness to learn.

In ballet, dancers are often encouraged to take risks and try new things, even if it means making mistakes. And the best dancers are those who are willing to learn from those mistakes and use them to improve their technique and artistry.

The same is true in leadership. Leaders who are willing to take calculated risks, try new approaches, and embrace failure as a learning opportunity are the ones who are most likely to succeed in the long run. They understand that mistakes are an inevitable part of the process and that the key to success is not avoiding failure but learning from it.

Let Go of Perfectionism

Perfectionism is a common trait among high achievers, but it can also be a hindrance to growth and success. Perfectionists often set impossibly high standards for themselves and can be overly critical when they don't meet those standards. This can lead to anxiety, burnout, and a reluctance to take risks or try new things.

In ballet, perfectionism can be particularly problematic. Dancers are often expected to strive for perfection in their technique and artistry, but this can lead to an unhealthy focus on flaws and mistakes. Instead of viewing mistakes as opportunities for growth, perfectionists may see them as evidence of their own inadequacy.

The same is true in leadership. Perfectionists may be hesitant to delegate tasks or trust others to take on important responsibilities because they fear that others won't meet their exacting standards. This can lead to micromanagement, burnout, and a lack of innovation and growth.

To truly embrace a growth mindset and let go of perfectionism, it's important to shift your focus from outcomes to process. Instead of striving for perfection, you can focus on progress and continuous improvement. This means being willing to take risks, try new things, and make mistakes along the way.

In ballet, this might mean experimenting with different interpretations of a role or trying a new technique, even if it means making mistakes in the process. By letting go of the need to be perfect and embracing the learning process, dancers can become more confident, versatile performers.

Leaders who are willing to take risks, try new approaches, and learn from their mistakes are the ones who are most likely to inspire their teams, foster innovation, and drive growth. By letting go of the need for perfection and embracing a growth mindset, leaders can become more effective, adaptive, and resilient.

Making mistakes is an essential part of the learning and growth process, both in ballet and in leadership. As Carol Dweck's research has shown, the most successful people are those who embrace a growth mindset and view mistakes as opportunities for learning and growth. By being willing to take risks, try new things, and learn from our failures, we become better dancers, better leaders, and better human beings.

Letting go of perfectionism is essential for growth and success, both in ballet and in leadership. By shifting our focus from outcomes to process, we can become more open to learning, more willing to take risks, and more resilient in the face of failure. So the next time you find yourself getting caught up in the pursuit of perfection, remember that it's okay to make mistakes and that those mistakes may be the very thing that helps you grow and succeed in the long run.

LESSON 13:

Throughout your lifetime, you're going to make mistakes. It's absolutely okay. We're human after all.

Rather than dwell and slip into a shame cycle, look at mistakes as a lesson. You don't have time to make ALL the mistakes. Learn from yours, and learn from others'.

Chapter 14

Courage and Kindness

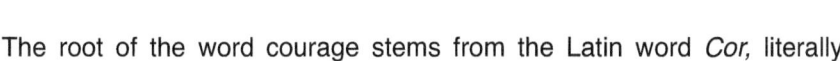

The root of the word courage stems from the Latin word *Cor,* literally meaning heart. To be kind and to show kindness requires heart.

In my first book, *Rise Of The Courageous Leader,* I share the nine Cs of courage and how for each one you need to "flex your courage muscle."

Courage *encourages* courage.

The more you try it out, the more you lean into the uncomfortableness of it, the more your capacity to experience discomfort grows and expands.

Courage is not the absence of fear, but rather the willingness to act in spite of fear.

It takes grit to be courageous, to push past your own limits and take risks that may feel uncomfortable or even frightening. As J.K. Rowling said,

"It takes a great deal of bravery to stand up to our enemies, but just as much to stand up to our friends."

Ballet dancers embody courage in many ways, from the physical demands of their art to the emotional and mental challenges they face in pursuit of their goals. They must push past their own physical limitations, training for hours each day to perfect their technique and performance. They must also navigate the competitive and often cutthroat world of professional dance, facing rejection and criticism on a regular basis.

Despite these challenges, ballet dancers remain committed to their art, driven by a passion and love for what they do. They have the courage to take risks, to push past their own fears and doubts, and to pursue their dreams with a relentless determination.

The lessons of courage that we learn from ballet and other disciplines can be applied to all aspects of our lives, including our personal and professional goals. As leaders, we must be willing to take risks, to push past our own fears and doubts, and to act with courage and conviction in pursuit of our vision.

But how do we cultivate courage in ourselves and others? One key factor is the relationship between courage and grit. Grit is the unyielding determination to push past our own limits and achieve excellence. It requires a level of discipline, focus, and perseverance that is critical to developing the courage necessary to take risks and pursue our goals.

Courage Encourages Courage

When we witness acts of courage in others, it inspires us to be more courageous ourselves. This is true in both personal and professional contexts. When we see a colleague take a risk and succeed, it gives us the courage to do the same. When we see a friend stand up for what they believe in, it inspires us to do the same.

However, developing courage requires a willingness to be kind to ourselves and others.

The amygdala, or the lizard brain, is the part of our brain that is responsible for our fight-or-flight response. It is wired to prioritise survival over all else, and can often lead us to make decisions based on fear rather than courage.

To develop courage, we must learn to work with our amygdala, rather than against it. This means being kind to ourselves and others, creating a safe and supportive environment that encourages risk-taking and growth. It means practising self-compassion, and recognising that failure and setbacks are an inevitable part of the growth process.

Ballet dancers understand the importance of kindness and support in their pursuit of excellence. They work in a highly competitive and demanding field, but they also rely on the support and encouragement of their colleagues and mentors to succeed. They know that it takes a village to achieve greatness, and they are willing to support and uplift each other along the way.

As a leader, you can apply these lessons of courage, grit, and kindness to our own leadership practices. You can create a culture of support and encouragement, where risk-taking and growth are celebrated rather than punished. You can prioritise self-compassion and kindness in your own leadership journey, recognising that the road to success is often paved with setbacks and failures.

Essentially, courage and grit are intimately linked, and both are critical to achieving excellence and success in our personal and professional lives. By cultivating a culture of support, kindness, and encouragement, we can inspire ourselves and others to act with courage and conviction, and to push past our own limits in pursuit of our goals.

Kindness

One of my personal values is kindness.

As the saying goes, "In a world where you can be anything, choose to be kind."

There's a common misconception that kindness is a weakness. This could not be further from the truth. There are enough people in the world who are having a hard time, there is plenty of unkind things going on, you only need to turn on the news.

You can be a strong leader, and still be kind. You can make tough decisions and be kind. You can be a strategic leader and be kind. You can be kind and say thank you.

Typically, success is often measured by wealth, power, and prestige. However, kindness is an essential component of grunt, grit, and grace, both in the ballet world and in leadership positions. For high achievers and high performers, kindness can be a powerful tool for building relationships, gaining trust, and achieving long-term success.

In ballet, kindness is essential for creating a positive and supportive environment. Dancers must work together as a team (corps de ballet), supporting each other through the rigours of training and performance. Often companies spend a lot of time together away from family and regular support networks.

Kindness towards fellow dancers, choreographers, performers, and artists can help build a culture of collaboration and respect, which can lead to greater success for the entire company.

Similarly, in leadership positions, kindness can be a powerful tool for building trust and respect. Kind leaders are seen as approachable and understanding and are more likely to foster a positive work environment. This can lead to better employee engagement, increased productivity, and greater success for the organisation as a whole.

For high achievers and high performers, kindness can be particularly challenging, as the pressure to succeed can sometimes lead to a focus on individual achievement at the expense of others. However, those who are able to cultivate kindness as a core value can reap the benefits of stronger relationships, greater trust, and more sustainable success over the long term.

Nice vs Kind

The distinction between being nice and being kind is often overlooked; as a leader it's essential to understand the differences. As a child you were probably told to "be nice" but what does that really mean?

Being nice involves pleasing others and being agreeable. If you have a tendency to please others, being nice comes naturally to you. It's about doing something helpful for others from a place of benevolence; however, being nice is often a product of societal conditioning and the expectations placed upon us.

While being nice allows people to stay comfortable, it doesn't necessarily bring about significant change or challenge the status quo. Let's consider an example: holding the door for someone. Is that an act of niceness or kindness? Well, it depends on your underlying intention. If you do it solely to create a favourable impression and expect something in return, it can be seen as a nice gesture. On the other hand, if your motivation is to spare the other person from inconvenience or extra effort, it becomes an act of kindness.

Kindness and niceness can be at odds with each other at times. For instance, telling an employee that they're struggling, or their performance is not up to scratch may not be considered nice, but it is a kind act if your intention is to help them improve.

"The standard you walk past is the standard you accept."

Similarly, calling out biases in a meeting may feel uncomfortable and not nice, but it is an act of kindness.

In some cases, even being overly cheerful can be unkind as it disregards the suffering of others and forces them to hide their true feelings in the name of niceness.

Brene Brown says it best, "clear is kind, unclear is unkind."

When it comes to choosing between kindness and niceness, Project Happiness firmly advocates for kindness. While niceness maintains a façade of having everything together and expects the same from others, kindness acknowledges that life can be challenging and embraces the emotional support we can provide.

Kindness allows for real success and failure, granting permission to be authentic and compassionate.

Many of my private clients suffer from "the disease to please" and are working to become recovering people pleasers. If you too are a recovering people pleaser I think it's time you start to prioritise kindness over niceness; by doing so, you can create an environment that recognises the complexities of life and encourages genuine connections and support.

Choose kindness, and make a positive difference in your leadership journey.

Being nice is often seen as a superficial, surface-level behaviour that is focused on being pleasant and agreeable to others. Nice leaders may avoid conflict or difficult conversations and prioritise keeping everyone happy, even if it means compromising their values, goals, or integrity.

On the other hand, being kind is rooted in empathy and a genuine desire to help others. Kind leaders take the time to understand their team members' needs, perspectives, and feelings, and use this understanding to guide their decisions and actions. They may still make difficult decisions or have tough conversations, but they do so with compassion and respect.

While being nice is focused on external behaviours and appearances, being kind is focused on internal motivations and genuine care for others. Kindness is an important virtue of grace in leadership, as it promotes trust, respect, and a positive team culture.

Being Nice	Being Kind
You bring your co-worker a cup of coffee in the morning, hoping to brighten their day.	A co-worker is going through a difficult time at home, and you offer to take on some of their workload so that they can have some space to deal with their personal issues.
You tell your team member they're doing a great job without offering any specific feedback or actionable advice.	A team member is struggling with a project, and you sit down with them to go through the work together and provide guidance and support.
You listen to your colleague vent about their workload, but you don't offer any suggestions or solutions.	A colleague is feeling overwhelmed and you offer to help them prioritise their tasks and come up with a plan to manage their workload more effectively.
You exchange polite small talk with the team member, but you don't go out of your way to engage with them further.	You notice that a team member seems to be struggling to connect with others, and you make an effort to include them in conversations and invite them to social events.
You overlook your co-worker's mistake and don't address it, even if it could impact the project's success.	A co-worker makes a mistake on a project, and you approach them with empathy and understanding, helping them figure out how to rectify the situation without assigning blame.

Kindness And Empathy Is A New Way of Leadership

As leaders when we suffer from empathy paralysis, we are unable to move past the feelings to the action. This stops us from tackling a more intentional, motivated, compassionate approach in our leadership. Having the ability to identify and feel someone's suffering may lead us to a deeper connection with that person. But if we can't act on it, then it can cloud our decision-making accuracy and our judgement as a leader.

Paul Bloom, author of *Against Empathy* and Professor of Cognitive Science and Psychology at Yale University, conducted a study to see if empathy can distort judgement. Two groups were asked to listen to a recording of a terminally ill child describing his pain. Group one was instructed to identify and feel for the child. On the other hand, group two was asked to listen objectively and not emotionally engage. Then each person was asked to decide if the child should be moved up a medically prioritised treatment list, giving benefits to that child, but potentially putting others more at risk.

The results showed that those who were emotionally connected to the child were more likely to move the child up the list even against professional medical opinions (three quarters of the group). However, of those who objectively listened to the child, only a third of the group made the same decision.

There are certainly benefits to taking action related to empathy. But there also seems to be a skill in having the right amount of empathy. This is the level that allows you to move through the empathy to the magic space where compassionate leadership shines.

Being intentional with your shift to demonstrating empathy (and sometimes compassion) is a proactive leadership choice that can benefit you in terms of the load you bear. But it is also highly beneficial to your team, giving them an open supportive space to voice concerns, challenges, and problems, as well as a psychologically safe space to sit with potential issues knowing that actionable solutions are at hand.

Layers of Care

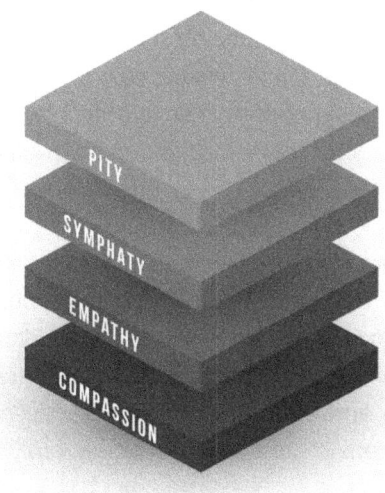

Pity

Pity really is the surface level of care. When we think about pity, it's really the level of care that is "I feel sorry for you."

Sympathy

Sympathy is your ability to understand someone's emption. Typically if we think of a sympathy card, we understand grief as a concept, however unless you've experienced this emotion yourself, the depth of understand is still quite surface level. Sympathy is "I feel you."

Empathy

Empathy is generally considered a virtue of grace. It involves the ability to understand and share the feelings of others, to put oneself in another's shoes, and to show compassion and concern for others. Empathy is often associated with the ability to connect with others on an emotional level, and to build strong, meaningful relationships. While empathy can be helpful in developing grit, which involves perseverance and resilience in the face of challenges, empathy itself is typically considered a key component of grace.

While it's true that as a leader you need to be emotionally intelligent and have the ability to empathise with your team as a whole as well as with individual members, it's compassion that allows you to take action on those empathetic emotions. It allows you to both identify with, but also lead through, empathy and sympathy, to drive outcomes that are beneficial for your team members, your team, and the entire organisation.

If you're unable to move through challenging moments that arise due to your empathy, you are at risk of developing "empathy fatigue" or sometimes called "compassion fatigue". Empathy fatigue happens when you rely too heavily on identifying with the emotions as opposed to identifying and then moving through them. And it results in traumatic stress and burnout that can create physical and mental exhaustion because your ability to cope with your everyday environment has been severely depleted.[1] That's no way to live ... or to lead.

Instead, we have to ensure that we don't rest in compassion but instead focus on leading with compassion.

Within empathy itself, there are three different levels:

1. Cognitive empathy—which is being aware of another person's emotional state.
2. Emotional empathy—which is engaging and sharing in those emotions.
3. Compassionate empathy—which is taking action to support other people.[2]

Empathy is another quality that seems to be getting more and more air time. In fact, I ran a leadership executive summit recently and one of our core topics was managing empathy and productivity.

[1] Cocker, F., Joss, Nerida. 'Compassion Fatigue among Healthcare, Emergency and Community Service Workers: A Systematic Review'. International Journal of Environmental Research and Public Health. June 2016. Accessed at https://www.ncbi.nlm.nih.gov/pmc/articles/PMC4924075/.
[2] 'Empathy at Work: Developing Skills to Understand Other People'. Mind Tools. Accessed at https://www.mindtools.com/pages/article/EmpathyatWork.htm#:~:text=Cognitive%20empathy%20is%20being%20aware,action%20to%20support%20other%20people.

For years, productivity and output have been the measure of successful leadership. However, with the disruption of COVID, and our new ways of working, empathy has supplanted output as a fundamental leadership skill that leaders need to lean into. That's not to say that output and outcomes are no longer important—they are. But what has changed is that output is no longer *at the expense* of empathy and compassion.

Years ago I was working with a dentist who said, "Ally, I don't really *do* empathy." As you can imagine, being a dentist he came into contact all day long with people who were highly anxious, in pain or otherwise upset and emotional. And while he didn't see empathy as an important part of his work, his patients certainly did. By not having this soft skill he lessened his desirability as a dentist, which meant an impact on his bottom line (something he could certainly understand). In his case, empathy was definitely a muscle that needed flexing.

Like this dentist, many leaders struggle with empathy. But in this case you actually *can* fake it until you make it. Begin by making the right noises, thinking about their perspective and considering how you might like to be treated if you were in their shoes. Over time you'll start to get a better sense of what your team might be feeling, and this will naturally develop and strengthen your empathy muscle.

Compassion

You're familiar with sympathy and empathy. But a basic human quality that we learn as children may be the key to moving us through emotionally-charged sympathy and empathy. And that key is compassion.

LESSON 14:

Kindness is contagious. In a world where you can be anything, choose
to be kind.

Act 2
Summary: Grit And Growth

Grit is the combination of passion and perseverance towards long-term goals. It's the ability to stay committed and focused on achieving what you set out to do, even in the face of setbacks and challenges. Growth mindset, on the other hand, is the belief that one's abilities and intelligence can be developed through hard work and dedication, rather than being fixed or predetermined. It's the willingness to embrace challenges and setbacks as opportunities for learning and growth, rather than as indicators of failure or inadequacy.

Together, grit and growth mindset can be powerful tools for success in any field. By cultivating a passion for what you do and staying committed to your goals, even in the face of adversity, you can build the resilience and determination needed to achieve great things. And by embracing a growth mindset and viewing failures and setbacks as opportunities for learning, you can continuously improve your skills and abilities, and achieve even greater success in the future.

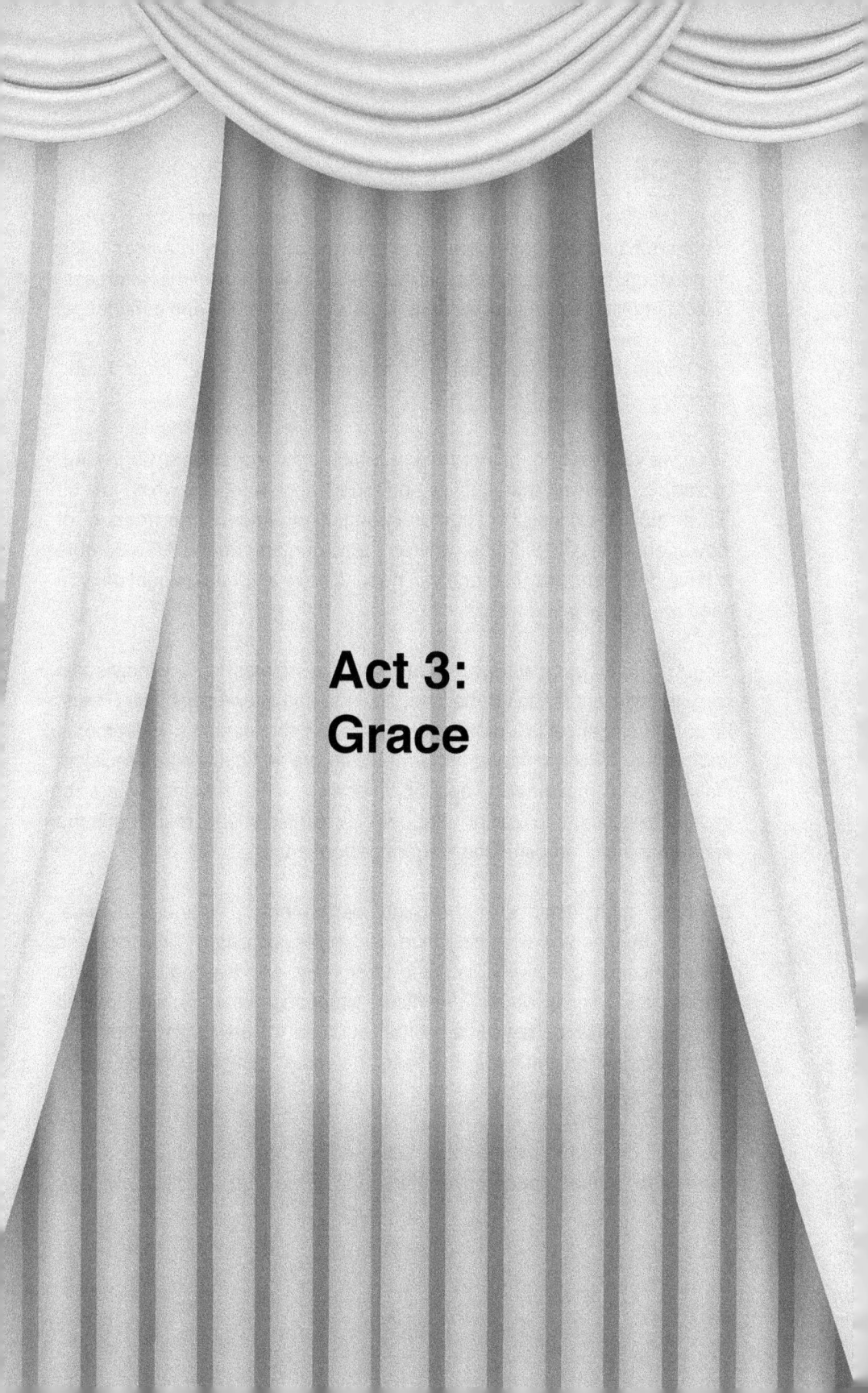

**Act 3:
Grace**

GRACE

Ally's definition—Grace is the finale. It's what all the work, the blood, sweat, and tears have been for. While in ballet terms this usually is a conclusion of a season. For leaders, grace is the ability to find leadership effortless. You can move through your leadership journey with poise and confidence.

Cambridge definition—A quality of moving in a smooth, relaxed, and attractive way.

So far we've gone through Act 1 Grunt, which is the root system, burrowing, spreading, providing that stability and foundation. Act 2 Grit which is a bit like a trunk, it's consistent, stands strong. And Grace is the freedom of movement of leaves with the wind and environment around it. To be able to have grace and stay in grace you need to have a strong foundation, you need roots to give you wings.

Elegance is an essential aspect of grace that relates to how individuals carry themselves in their behaviour, actions, and interactions with others. In ballet, elegance is demonstrated through the dancer's movements and posture, which must be performed with grace, fluidity, and precision, making their movements appear effortless. This requires years of training, practice, and discipline to perfect their technique, resulting in the appearance of a graceful and elegant performance.

Similarly, high achievers and high performers in leadership must conduct themselves with elegance and professionalism. This involves communicating effectively, listening attentively, and treating others with respect and dignity, even in difficult situations. Leaders who exhibit elegance in their behaviour are often admired for their poise, tact, and diplomacy, which enables them to navigate complex interpersonal relationships with ease.

Elegance in leadership is also reflected in how individuals present themselves in their appearance, attire, and demeanour. Additionally, their speech, body language, and conduct must be professional, calm, and composed, demonstrating their confidence and credibility.

Overall, elegance as a virtue of grace is essential for individuals to conduct themselves with poise, grace, and professionalism in their interactions with others. It allows individuals to navigate complex interpersonal relationships with ease, exuding confidence and credibility, which is critical for those 23%er who are high achievers and high performers in leadership.

Plant a Tree

I love the old adage of *The best time to plant a tree was 10 years ago, the next best time is right now.* My wish for leaders is for them to give themselves some grace.

It's important to recognise that there's a difference between grace and being graceful. In this context, grace is around poise and how you display yourself as a leader, your disposition. Graceful is how you carry about your role as a leader. It's about uplifting others around you. It's about elevating each moment and opportunity and recognising how short and beautiful life really is.

Leaders need to give themselves some grace. If you dropped a ball, perhaps all the balls, it's okay; just walk back to where you dropped them, pick them up, and carry on.

The ultimate image of grace is a graceful ballerina. The seeming effortlessness to move across a stage, the transition from one step to the next, and from one scene to the next. The keyword here is seeming. Behind the scenes and backstage, there are ballerinas madly running from one side of the stage to the next, costume changes happening at a lightning speed, and bloody blisters being taped and bandaged before stepping into the spotlight as graceful as can be.

Leadership can be downright chaotic. That chaos can consume you, or you can control your response and reaction.

Chapter 15

The Virtues of Grace

It's taken years of experience and reflection to understand and appreciate the importance of grace in leadership.

In Chapter 3 I discussed comparison, and I wanted to touch on it again in grace.

Often seen as soft skills these are actually the power skills that can elevate your leadership. The number one thing stopping leaders from making that transition to executive level is trust. It's a tough pill to swallow. Building trust, leading with trust and psychological safety. Here are some of the things you can use to build trust.

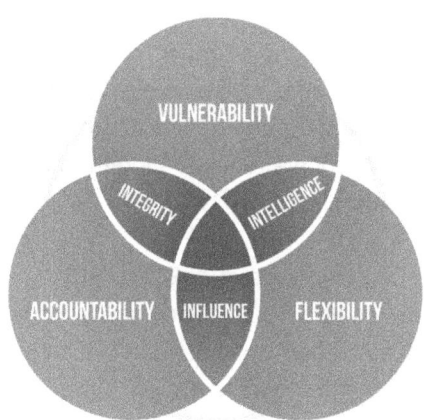

Vulnerability

What we think about when it comes to vulnerability in the workplace is the need to air our dirty laundry, share all aspects of our life, and our shortcomings with those that lead. Whilst this may be engaging and sometimes entertaining, this is not what vulnerability actually is. Vulnerability is our ability to connect with people through a shared experience. It is our ability to share a time that was perhaps deeply painful. It's putting trust in the persons we're sharing with to hold that space for us.

Vulnerability needs honesty; can you share your story honestly? Vulnerability needs care; there's risk-taking involved in sharing with someone. Vulnerability is putting the ego away and learning from mistakes and then implementing those learnings without spiralling into a shame spiral.

Flexibility

Flexibility is a highly valuable quality for both personal and professional success. In the context of trust, being flexible means being adaptable to changing circumstances and being open to different perspectives and ideas. When you demonstrate flexibility in your relationships, you show that you are willing to work with others and that you can be trusted to adjust your behaviours and approaches when necessary.

In the context of winning a seat at the table, flexibility is also crucial. It means being able to pivot and adapt to changing business needs and being open to new ideas and approaches. When leaders demonstrate flexibility, they inspire confidence in their teams and stakeholders, who know that the leader is capable of navigating through uncertain times and adapting to new challenges.

However, it's important to note that flexibility shouldn't be confused with being wishy-washy or indecisive. Being flexible doesn't mean compromising on core values or making decisions based solely on the opinions of others. Instead, flexibility means being open to new information and being willing to adjust course when necessary, while still maintaining a clear sense of direction and purpose.

Overall, flexibility is an essential quality for leaders who want to build trust and win a seat at the table. By demonstrating the ability to adapt and pivot in the face of change, leaders can inspire confidence and build strong relationships with their teams and stakeholders.

Flexibility involves the ability to adapt to new situations, change course when necessary, and approach challenges with an open mind. This requires a certain degree of vulnerability, as it means being willing to step outside of one's comfort zone and take risks. Vulnerability, in turn, can be an expression of grace, as it involves being open and receptive to new experiences and perspectives.

In terms of winning a seat at the table, flexibility can be a key asset for high performers and high achievers. Those who are able to demonstrate flexibility in their thinking and approach to problem-solving may be more likely to be viewed as valuable assets to an organisation or team. Additionally, the ability to be flexible can help build trust with colleagues, as it demonstrates a willingness to work collaboratively and find solutions that benefit everyone involved.

Accountability

There's been a whirlwind of discussions since the return to the post-pandemic workplace, and one topic that continues to resurface is accountability. I've heard statements like "I wish our leaders were more accountable" and "finding accountable people is a real challenge." It's evident that accountability plays a vital and pivotal role in our work and team dynamics and it's closely tied to trust, reliability, and responsibility.

When it comes to grace, I define accountability to mean taking ownership and being willing to answer for your actions (and mistakes). In the workplace, it's a fundamental quality that shapes the culture and team dynamics. It might sound straightforward, but the real question is, why do we often struggle with accountability, both as individuals and leaders?

From my experience, people usually deliberately shirk accountability. More often, it's due to a lack of understanding—whether it's unclear expectations or a vague sense of what's required in their roles. Additionally, limited resources and unrealistic timelines can create hurdles, all of which stem from a lack of effective communication.

As a leader, you must ask yourself and your teams: is personal accountability a guiding value in our part of the business? It's crucial to build trust among team members, and that trust is intertwined with accountability. Without accountability, you can't truly lead and your teams wont thrive.

So, how do you create a culture of accountability within your team? The first step is acknowledging that we all have areas we may lack discipline.

Embracing accountability doesn't mean you're perfect, it means you're committed to doing better and holding yourself and others accountable.

Accountability is the key to moving from intentions to actions. Often, people have good intentions but struggle to follow through. Accountability bridges that gap, making sure your actions align with what you intend(ed) to do.

I believe that the moment you hold yourself accountable, something changes within you. It's like a switch that turns on your drive to do better, to achieve your goals, and to be responsible for your actions. When you become accountable to yourself and to others, you unlock your true potential as a leader.

Accountability is a core aspect of effective leadership and team dynamics; it underpins the three virtues of grace. By embodying accountability, you can build trust in yourself, and others, improve leaders, lead by example. By embracing accountability as the bridge that propels us from intention to action, you can inspire your team to do the same.

The 3 I's of Grace

Intelligence

Intelligence is really recognising whether you have a strong work ethic is really around are you keeping your promises to others to do the work that you said you were going to do? Are you giving it your best effort, and can you give the same rigour to the boring and mundane as you can the exciting and glittery work?

Integrity

Integrity is really what kind of character you have. It's the tapestry of how you conduct yourself and what you stand for and what you stand against. To have and demonstrate integrity you need a strong work ethic, focus, conviction, and my favourite—all roads lead to the high road.

Influence

Influence is built upon a foundation of trust.
A leader who is not trusted has a limited ability to create and use influence.
So it's important to focus on *doing* right, rather than *being* right.

When you don't just talk the talk but walk the walk, then you build trust.
People will rarely make a leap of faith for someone who hasn't earned
their trust.

All Roads Lead to the High Road

As Michelle Obama said, when they go down, we go up. And I think
Michelle Obama was not only a first lady full of grace, she was also right on
so many levels. Going down is easy, meeting someone to defend yourself,
or getting into pettiness is easy. Taking the high road is much harder. It's
about doing what's right, rather than doing what's easy.

LESSON 15:

In the world of leadership, it's equally crucial for leaders to grant themselves a health dose of grace. In my experience working closely with my private clients, I've come across highly ambitious, and driven individuals who are making remarkable progress in their leadership journeys. however it's all too common for them to be their worst critic and harshly criticise themselves for not knowing everything they think they should.

I often remind them of perhaps one of the most challenging leadership lessons of all - learning to sit with, embrace and acknowledge their own humanity. It's about realising that we are human *beings*, not just human *doings*. So it's not only acceptable, but also vital to extend grace to themselves in this demanding lifelong pursuit of leadership excellence.

Chapter 16

Flow and Freedom

Early in my parenting journey, I read somewhere that for children to be able to spread their wings, you need to give them roots.

The same is true for grace; the grunt is the root system, burrowing, spreading, and providing that stability and foundation. The grit is a bit like a trunk; it's consistent and stands strong. And grace is the freedom of movement of leaves with the wind and environment around it. To be able to have grace and stay in grace, you need to have a strong foundation, you need roots to give you wings.

Flow State

As a dancer during performance season, it's not uncommon to learn and rehearse a two-and-a-half-hour performance multiple times in a day and then several performances in a day across a week or a month. My friends used to always ask, how could I remember all the steps to each show. I had a special technique that worked for me. If I could run through the entire thing in my mind from start to finish, it only ever needed to be the one piece of music/dance, then I knew with 100% certainty that I'd committed that dance to memory. If on the other hand I couldn't run through the whole thing in my mind without distraction, then there was still work to do.

Once I realised this was my key to getting into flow state it became much easier to remember each of the pieces. To this day if there's classical music in a shopping centre I can remember each of the steps to each count of the music. I can't remember to collect my mail, but I can remember a routine from 15 years ago that I'll never need to perform again. It's funny the things we hold on to.

Recently I've been looking into flow and how to get into flow state. If you're not familiar with Csikszentmihalyi's work on how we can experience enjoyment in our lives, I highly recommend you add it to your reading list.

Freedom

I think flow and freedom go hand in hand. As someone who continually seeks freedom, freedom from rules, conformity, and status quo, I find it useful to have structure to my freedom. Freedom gives the flexibility to move, pivot, pirouette even. As a leader, your ability to adapt and change will be key to your success.

Grace is a little bit like the payoff. It's the glory shot, it's making all that effort, the blood, sweat, and tears worth it. Grace is the standing ovation, the encore, and the confirmation of all the reasons you put in the hard work.

Permission for Grace

It's interesting when I work with exceptional leaders, the number of times they know what they need to do, they know they're good enough, but they're waiting for someone to give them permission. They're waiting for a permission slip to shoot for the moon. Here's the thing, the only person who can give you permission to shine bright is you yourself. No one else needs to *let* you shine bright.

Permission for grace is recognising that it's not going to be perfect all the time; in fact, being perfect would mean there's been a stagnation of growth.

I was working with a client who mentioned she didn't like a particular IT system she was introducing. My response to her was, "*Do you have to like it for it to be effective?*" The answer, of course was, "*No, I don't need to like it for it to*

be effective." Letting go of the need for everything to be perfect gives you the freedom to move the effort where you can get the most bang for your buck.

People Pleaser

Are you a people pleaser... The compulsion to please others, often referred to as the "disease to please," is a common but often overlooked issue that can have significant consequences on your well-being, personal growth and leadership reputation. Many people are driven by an innate desire for approval and have an irrational fear of rejection. They find themselves trapped in a perpetual cycle of people-pleasing, often at the expense of their own needs and desires.

This insidious behaviour pattern can manifest in various aspects of life, from personal relationships to professional endeavours. People who fall victim to this 'disease' are often the ones who have difficulty saying no, fearing that declining a request or expressing their true opinions might upset or disappoint others. They expend an excessive amount of energy and emotional resources trying to meet everyone's expectations (near impossible), often at the cost of their own happiness and authenticity.

The root of this issue often lies in a deep-seated need for external validation and a fear of confrontation or disapproval. Leaders who grapple with people-pleasing tend to prioritise the comfort and happiness of others over their own, neglecting their own needs and desires in the process. They become trapped in a relentless cycle of seeking approval, which can erode their self-esteem and lead to feelings of emptiness and resentment. Most importantly, they are rarely aware of the level and degree to which they apologies unnecessarily.

Breaking free from the "disease to please" is a journey towards self-empowerment. It involves recognising and valuing your own needs and boundaries, learning to assert yourself, and being aware of the impact the language is having on your confidence, and outward perspective. It's essential for leaders who find themselves caught in this pattern to take some action, reclaim their agency and prioritise their own well-being (and agenda).

Individuals who can break free from the shackles of people-pleasing, cultivate healthier, more fulfilling relationships with themselves and others.

In short, stop saying sorry all the time.

Things to stop saying sorry for immediately:

- Being busy and owning your time
- Setting boundaries for yourself
- Not being perfect
- Showing emotions... having emotions
- Not being able to read minds
- Needing help
- Taking up space

Turn Shame into Gratitude

It's time to overcome the need to constantly apologise. Here are some key phrases I use in our Communication Workshops, and with my private clients.

Save your 'sorrys' for when it's really necessary. It'll be more sincere.

Instead of this....	Say this....
Sorry I'm late	Thanks for waiting for me
Sorry I missed that (if someone finds an error in your work)	Nice pick up, thanks for letting me know
Sorry for talking so much	Thank you for listening to me
Sorry for being so sensitive	Thank you for being accepting of me
Sorry I can't make it to XX	Thank you for inviting me
Sorry, I forgot!	Thanks for reminding me.
Sorry for bothering you	Thank you for your attention.
I just want to check in (on work you're waiting for, that's probably over due)	When can I expect to receive an update on X

Replace "But" with "And"

As an NLP practitioner, I understand the importance of language, and how the language we use change your internal state. This is a great trick to reframe if you disagree with someone or something, or you've got yourself stuck in a thinking rut.

When you hear the word **but**, replace it with the word **and**.

For example:

a). Yes, **but** here's another thing to consider
b). Yes, **and** here's another thing to consider

a). I'd love to go to the event, **but** I get anxious
b). I'd love to go to the event, **and** I get anxious.

a). You make a valid point, **but** I have some reservations about the proposed budget
b). You make a valid point, **and** I have some reservations about the proposed budget

a). I respect your opinion, **but** I believe the market research suggests a different approach
b). I respect your opinion, **and** I believe the market research suggests a different approach

a). I understand your perspective, **but** I have a different interpretation of the data
b). I understand your perspective, **and** I have a different interpretation of the data

a). You've done great work, **but** there are still a few issues we need to address
b). You've done great work, **and** there are still a few issues we need to address

a). I respect your decision, **but** I believe we should revisit this issue in the future

b). I respect your decision, **and** I believe we should revisit this issue in the future

a). I value your input, **but** I think we should consider alternative strategies.

b). I value your input, **and** I think we should consider alternative strategies.

Statement *a* which includes the 'but' dismisses the comment or sentence before the but, makes the statement argumentative and dismissive.

Statement *b* allows further communication and understanding while acknowledging and validating the beginning comment.

Busy vs Productive

In my 20 years of experience working as a leader and with leaders, I'm yet to be told that someone has too much time. Typically I hear things like, if only I had an extra hour a day. I could probably get on top of things if I had more time.

When I work with teams and leaders, I like to set them a challenge. That challenge is to replace the word 'busy' with 'productive'. For two weeks following the workshop or masterclass, they commit to using productive (or a variation of) rather than busy.

The result? Miraculous, all of a sudden, they're not spending hours (and hours) busy in email... because honesty, who's ever been productive on email. All or a sudden they're re-evaluating what their calendar looks like, and reassessing what is 'busy work' and what is really going to move the needle. If you've been stuck in a busy rut, I'd encourage you to have a look at your language, and mark the calendar for your own two week challenge.

If you would like to join the 'busy challenge' head to www.madeformore.com.au/resources

LESSON 16:

Language is important, what you say, and what you hear yourself say is important. Language plays a vital role in your personal confidence and your leadership reputation, especially if you've been in the habit of continually apologising.

Overusing phrases like I'm sorry can erode your self-esteem. By consciously reframing your language (and your thinking) and reserving your apologies for when they're genuinely warranted will help you regain your confidence, and and project leadership gravitas.

It's a transformative shift that not only boosts confidence, but also enhances your leadership presence and credibility too.

Chapter 17

Poise and Positioning

--- ★ ⭐ ★ ---

How do you want to carry yourself with grace through life? How do you want to show up as a leader?

Be, Do, Have

Within my business our tagline is Be More, Do More, Achieve More.

Often we start out thinking we need to have something, usually triggered by a title in leadership: I can't lead until I'm the leader. Then that will allow us to "do" certain things. Once I'm a "leader" then I'll be able to "do" the things, once I can "do" the things, I'll "be" more confident, taken seriously, and understand what's going on here.

NLP technique works in the reverse; instead of Have, Do, then Be, what if you were to Be, Do, Have?

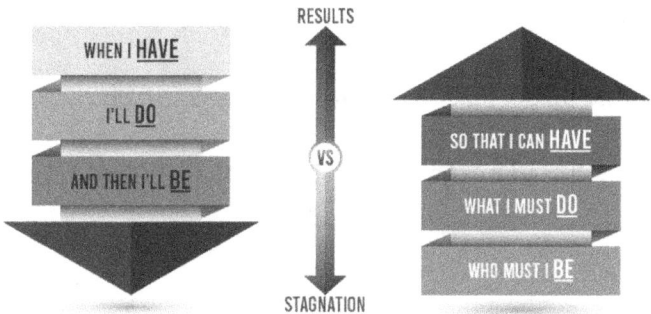

Be more confident; be serious enough to be taken seriously, Do the things (after all, the only permission slip you're waiting on is your own). Have the title. It's often said that for leaders to make that next step, they are already demonstrating a number of the skills, competencies, and attributes required for the role.

Poise Under Pressure

I can remember numerous times throughout my career when I need to keep poise under pressure.

1. On stage waiting for the curtain to open for the final act only having just changed costumes, toes bleeding, having to fill in for someone who had injured themselves and desperately needing to pee. Perhaps it's the showbiz of "the show must go on."

2. Early in my leadership journey having to present to exec about a project we were looking to get and significantly change some processes which would save time and money, and would also mean staff redundancies; after presenting my part of the presentation, and sitting on the side of the stage waiting for the rest of my team to finish their bit. When I went to walk back onstage my leg that was crossed had gone completely dead. I couldn't feel it at all, and as I hobbled/limped onto the stage with one foot in a high heel, and the other foot walking on my ankle, I pretended nothing was wrong. What a dill!

I think poise is inherently linked to posture, and how we feel internally and energetically. Cleaning up the emotional turmoil inside is key to having poise under pressure.

A Brené Brown quote that has always resonated so highly with me is

"Don't shrink, don't puff up, stand your sacred ground."

When leaders stand in their power, can maintain poise under pressure, there's a magic that happens. In these instances, I'd encourage you to fake it till you make it. I don't mean fake your capability; I mean fake your self-belief until you begin to believe it yourself.

Poise, they say, is a self-possessed assurance. A technique I use with my clients who are looking to present better go through our Presentation Skills Masterclass and will practice poise. Amy Cuddy's famous TED talk on Power Poses is just one example of how leaders can get into the right state of mind purely through posture.

Beyoncé, who was incredibly stage shy (can you believe it!?), created an alter ego Sasha Fierce who went on stage, and thank goodness she did because we truly would've missed out on her incredible talent.

If you are looking at how you can step into your power with poise even under pressure, imagine which version of you you would need to be to feel comfortable to do that. Step into your own alter ego (make sure you give yourself a very cool name), step into your belief, trust that you have learned what you need to learn.

"The map is not the terrain."

You past experiences do not predict your future. Ask yourself, what could go right with this?

Shoulders Back, Chin Up, Eyes Ahead

There's a lot to be said about the way we move and present ourselves in space. When I work with leaders many of them are battling the itty bitty shitty committee, that internal monologue that's not helpful, telling them they're not good enough, what they have to say may be rubbish.

I distinctly remember the feeling standing in the wings on the side of stage waiting for my cue to step out. A key learning from my dancing days is you're presenting before anyone can see you. We didn't wait to step onto stage before we were in character and performing; no, that happened in the wings to prepare our body, and our state of mind.

When I was studying to become and accredited NLP (neurolinguistic programming) practitioner, I learnt the importance of looking up, (from a neurological perspective). Where we look can directly impact our thought patterns; specifically, if we're looking down, more often than not there is negative talk going on. If we're looking up and out, it's much harder to access those negative thoughts.

Below is an image of the *standard* eye direction for many people. Keeping in mind this is of course not going to be a one-size-fits-all based on personal preferences, which is your dominant side, etc. However, if you're interested in knowing more about accessing this deeper level of understanding, reach out to an NLP practitioner to help identify your patterning.

- Visual Constructed (VC), eyes move to the left-upper corner.
- Visual Remembered (VR), eyes move to the right-upper corner.
- Audio Constructed (AC), eyes move horizontally to the left.
- Audio Remembered (AR), eyes move horizontally to the right.
- Feelings (K) and body sensations, eyes move to the lower left.
- Internal Dialogue (AD), eyes move to the lower right.

We each hold a unique model of the world around us. There is an old saying that eyes are the windows to the soul, and perhaps a better way to understand this is that eyes are the gateway to accessing the realms of the mind. The way your eyes move, also known as eye accessing cues, illuminate specific corners of your brain as if they are messengers connecting to your deepest thoughts. Imagine posing a question such as, "How does it feel to be drenched in rain?" While processing that question, your eyes will embark on a quest darting through the halls and memory bank of your mind in search of the answer. Each movement of your eyes triggers a cascade of activity, lighting up various regions of your brain as it seeks the truth. It's an intricate dance, an interplay of cognition and curiosity.

Visual construct (Vc)

This is where the mind weaves images and constructs scenes from the depths of your imagination, where you generate a mental picture. When someone moves their eyes up and to the left (for many, but not always all) it indicates they are accessing an image that needs to be freshly constructed as it may not have been seen before or stored in the immediate recall zone of the mind. This could be something along the lines of if someone asked you "What would your kitchen look like if it was purple with yellow polka dots?"; in response to that type of question your mind engages in a creative dance to conjure up a vivid picture of a purple-themed kitchen which may not exist in reality, but emerges from the realm of possibilities.

Visual remembered (Vr)

Visual remembered is the process of accessing previously seen or imagined images in the mind's eye. When someone moves their eyes up and to the right, (typically) it indicates they are retrieving visual memories from their consciousness. This might include recalling colours, objects, and scenes such as childhood room colours, the number of chairs in a room or recalling your first bike. Engaging in visual remembered allows for introspection and can strengthen our ability to recall memories and gain insight into our personal history.

Audio construct (Ac)

Audio construct involves accessing new sounds and constructing imaginative auditory experiences within the mind. When someone shifts their attention laterally and to the left, they can create unique sounds or conversations that may not have been heard before. Engaging in audio construct allows individuals to explore sonic adventures, envisioning scenarios like mimicking Donald Duck or imagining how a cat would sound barking. (Think about any of the "secret sound" segments on mainstream radio). Through audio construct the mind's ear can transform the familiar into the fantastical.

Audio remembered (Ar)

Audio remembered involves retrieving familiar sounds and conversations stored in the mind's auditory memory. Shifting attention laterally and to the right triggers the recollection of various auditory experiences, includes past conversations, voice (both your own and others'), and recognisable sounds from different sources. Engaging in audio remembered exercises allows individuals to immerse themselves in a sonic archive of moments. By asking questions like "What was the very last thing I said?" "Can you remember when you first heard your favourite song?" you can relive recent conversations and evoke the comfort of a nostalgic moment.

Feelings or kinaesthetic (K)

Kinaesthetic involves accessing internal emotions and external tactile sensations. When the mind's focus shifts downward and to the left (typically) it allows us to explore a wide range of feelings, both emotional and physical, stored within our consciousness. By asking questions like "What does it feel like to swim in water?" you can tap into tactile sensations. The power of feeling or kinaesthetic lies in your ability to connect you to the intricacies of your emotional landscape and sensory experience.

Internal dialogues or auditory digital (Ad)

This is the big one I want you to tune into. Auditory digital is the key piece when we're looking at poise. Auditory digital allows us to explore our self-talk and inner dialogue. When our eyes move down and to the right, (typically) we gain access to the stream of thoughts and mental chatter that accompanies us throughout the day. Typically the leaders that I work with don't have helpful positive mental chatter.

When looking to access grace, with poise, it's important to look up and out, and disengage from the negative internal dialogue.

Reframing

As an NLP practitioner I understand the power of reframing, for myself as well as for my clients and students. When leaders tap into the magic of reframing it completely elevates their ability to lead and coach their people.

Reframing is your ability to look at something from a different perspective. This is often used to look at something that might at first be considered negative and then reframed in a positive way.

Reframing is a really important skill to learn, not only for yourself but also to help your team. If you think about it, the way to speak (and talk to yourself) is really important. Words are so powerful. And the person you're listening to the most is YOU. So make sure what you're telling yourself is helpful.

Being able to reframe a situation allows you to look at it from another perspective.

Here are some of the common reframes I like to use.

What's the problem?	What are possible solutions?
I don't know how	I'll seek guidance and learn how to do it
I'm all over the place.	I'm good at a lot of things.
What can I get?	What can I give?
I can't do that	Let's explore alternative solutions
That's impossible	It's a challenging task, let's find a way
That's not my job	I can direct you to the right person
I hate this task	This doesn't energise me, but I'll tackle it
I'm too busy for this	I have a full schedule and I'll make time for it
I've always done it that way	Let's explore hat options could be possible
It's not my fault	I'll take responsibility and work on a solution
I don't have time for training	I'll find time to improve my skills
I don't want to take on more responsibility	I'm open to discussing how we can mange additional tasks
I don't like feedback	I welcome constructive feedback for personal and professional growth
I can't work with them	I'll work to find a common ground and build rapport
I don't want to learn new tech	I'm interested to stay updated with the latest trends.

The Cartesian Quadrant

Sometimes the most difficult challenge for leaders is to know which is the best decision to make at the time. I like to use this tool to help look at options for different perspectives.

The four questions are:
What would happen if I did? What would happen if I didn't, what wouldn't happen if I did? What wouldn't happen if I didn't?

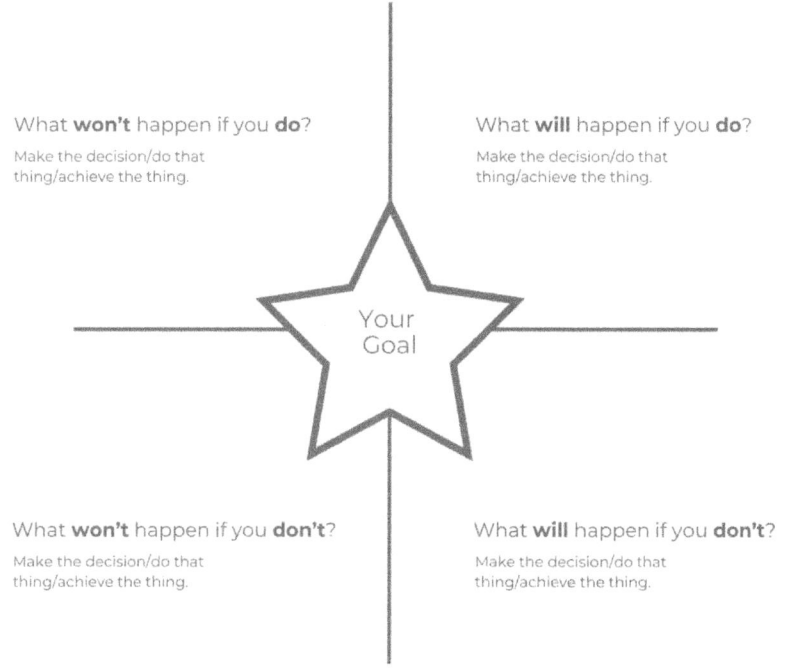

What **won't** happen if you **do**?
Make the decision/do that thing/achieve the thing.

What **will** happen if you **do**?
Make the decision/do that thing/achieve the thing.

Your Goal

What **won't** happen if you **don't**?
Make the decision/do that thing/achieve the thing.

What **will** happen if you **don't**?
Make the decision/do that thing/achieve the thing.

Leadership Gravitas

When I think about my time on the stage, there were dancers that just had *"it"* and others who were technically great but you may not have noticed them. When I think about what it was that really made some performers stand out in the crowd (or corps-de-ballet), it was the ones that had presence. They held themselves like they belonged there. They moved with confidence and grace, you couldn't not notice them.

When I'm working with leaders now, what they're looking for is "executive presence," or executive gravitas. I think it's a combination of these three elements that helps leaders with not only their poise but also their presence.

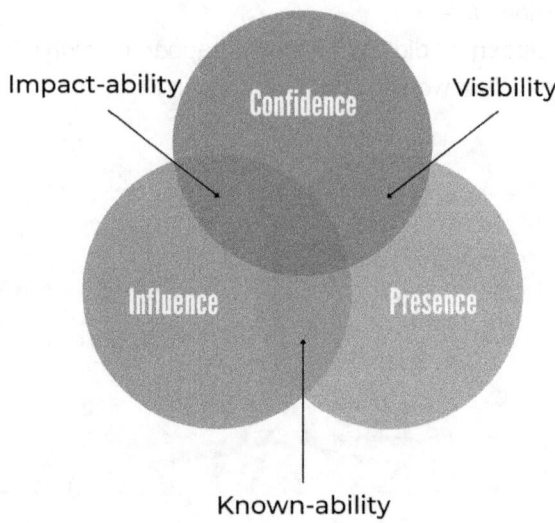

LESSON 17:

Eyes up, look ahead to where you're going. Step into your space and own it.

Chapter 18

Reflect and Refine

The Elusive Pursuit For Perfection

One of the most painful yet fruitful activities as a professional dancer was to watch the recording; each lesson, each rehearsal and performance was an opportunity to reflect on where there could be improvement. Was the timing out, could the extension be a little more, the jumps a little higher? What worked, why did it work, and could we recreate it?

Throughout my leadership journey there have been teams that perform well, and some that quite frankly do not. As a leader, that constant pursuit for high performance, what does it look like, how to you cultivate it, and if it's already working, how can you bottle it or reproduce it?

Stop, Start, Continue

One of the most powerful practices leaders can adopt is the simple act of reflection. Whether the cadence is weekly, monthly, or quarterly. Squaring out the time to reflect on what activities, behaviours, and thoughts need to stop. What's spinning the wheels and getting you nowhere, what activities, behaviours, or thoughts could you start? What is something new that you could try out? What needs to continue? What is going well and can be either amplified, systemised or outsourced or delegated?

The Chinese Bamboo Theory

When I first started my leadership and communication consultancy— Made For More—I engaged a coach early on who talked about Chinese bamboo. You see, Chinese bamboo spends the early part of its life growing a vast, diverse root system underground with nothing to be seen by the naked eye for months, sometimes years. Then, seemingly overnight, bamboo shoots pop up all over the place.

Grace is very similar to this bamboo. Those who are looking in from the outside see the poise, the ease, without realising the grunt and grit that has happened prior for the strong root system to allow this grace.

The Woodchopper and the Axe

One of the biggest lessons I've learned over time is the benefits of *slowing down to speed up*. In ballet this looked like set recovery days, in leadership this might look like taking days off, and in personal life this has become well known as well-being.

There's a brilliant fable that I'd like to share with you. It's about two woodchoppers.

Once upon a time in a village far away, there was a woodchopper, and he had been chopping wood for 60+ years and was well known throughout the lands as the best wood chopper of all time. One day a young and eager man came along, and challenged the old wood chopper to a competition. The old man accepted the challenge. Word spread throughout the village far and wide that there was going to be a wood chopping challenge.

Both men started the day chopping their wood. As the sun was high in the sky, both men had been chopping wood for hours; they were sweaty and getting tired. Both had equal amounts of wood by this time. At about lunchtime, the old man stopped chopping his wood, and wandered into the forest.

The young woodchopper noticed and thought now was the time to really go for it, and set about chopping wood with new rigour. An hour or so later the wood chopper came back and continued to chop his wood.

At the end of the day, the competition had finished; each of the men had spent the whole day chopping wood with the exception of the old man's time when he wandered into the forest.

When they tallied up the wood, the old man had won. The young wood chopper was furious; how could this be? He hadn't had a break all day; in fact, he was exhausted.

He approached the old man and questioned if he had cheated somehow, and how he could possibly have won when he'd spent an hour in the woods.

The old man looked at the young man and said, "When I went into the woods, I spent that time sitting, resting and sharpening my axe."

He slowed down to rest, regroup, and sharpen his tool.

When was the last time you took time out to slow down so you could speed up?

Slow Down to Speed Up

Some of the work I love to do that has huge ongoing impact is work with teams on their strategy and planning days.

So often, I'm told by leaders that they don't have time to do the strategic work, they don't have time to delegate, and train their people, they don't have time to plan because they're busy being busy.

Successful leaders and teams know the power of a good planning session, and the importance of taking time out of their day/week/month to develop a clear plan.

Having a look at the matrices below, where we spend our time matters. So often we're spending too much time in the doing, and not enough time in the planning.

 **DO**

Identify what's important that needs attention now. Time chunk these activities and tasks.

15%-25%

 **DEFER**

Book time in your calendar to carve out time and space to complete this activity or task

60%-85%

 **DELEGATE**

What knowledge can you share with your team to upskill as well as free up your time.

15%-25%

 **DELETE**

Stop doing anything noisy - that makes you 'busy' but not 'productive'.

0%

"An hour of planning can save you 10 hours of doing."
Dale Carnegie

When I work with leaders, often they're looking for more time and ways to work more efficiently. I think leaders should be trying to make themselves redundant. In fact, I think the ultimate measure of success for a leader is that their team is operating so well, they can go on leave without things falling to pieces, and they can take time out to focus on strategy or what we call 'working ON the business'.

You might be thinking, this sounds amazing, and also, a little far-fetched. The secret ingredient to a high-performing team is not outsourcing work or doing it all yourself but empowering the people you have in your current team.

Here are the reasons why empowerment is the way to go.

1. Let it go (think Elsa from *Frozen*)
    Empowerment is a leadership code for letting go of some responsibilities and giving them to the brilliantly talented people within your team.

    This might feel like it's hard for many leaders, especially if you're used to wearing all of the hats or being the technical expert within your team.

    Sometimes you need to slow down to speed up.

    If you learn to empower your staff, you create the space and mental clarity to work on your strategic thinking and the next steps for your area of responsibility.

    As your team take on more responsibilities, they inevitably take work off your plate as well as upskilling at the same time.

    Plus, (and I say this with kindness) you will probably not be the best in everything you do within your team. There are things that are not in your genius zone. Or maybe you're good at it but you don't like doing it.

    Look for people that love doing those things you can't or don't want to do. Then assign (code for delegate) those tasks so you can concentrate on the things you can or love to do.

    At the end of the day, isn't that what being a leader is all about? You focus on the big picture and lead your staff to take charge of the parts that make the vision a reality.

    A good rule of thumb is to think about where you're spending your time. You want to spend the most amount of time in the "Defer" quadrant. This includes things like Planning, Strategic Thinking, Professional Development and Training, and the least amount of time in the "Delete"

quadrant; this is things like spending too much time in emails, socials media, making spreadsheets look good, etc.

2. Encourage different ideas
   Don't be afraid to collect people around you who have radical ideas that you might never have thought of.

   People who work in a creative space actually use all parts of their brains. This happens because the different ideas and perspectives fire off different synapses within everyone's brain.

   Encourage your people to share their big, hairy, audacious ideas that could spell a win-win situation for your team.

3. Paint the big picture (macro thinking)
   Your team will trust your decisions to positively impact them. But at times, they expect to feel empowered to make those important decisions that directly or indirectly affect them.

   You don't have to throw them into the deep end and leave them to fend for themselves.

   Communication is key.

   Share a clear picture of your vision with them. Then, collaborate on what they can achieve, what will be a stretch in terms of learning and timeframes, and develop the next steps together.

LESSON 18:

As a dancer, you always start at the barré, even the best of the best start there. Because it's all in the warm up and the preparation.

The same applies for your leadership journey. To have a formidable career, you need to have a strong foundation. Slow down, to speed up.

Chapter 19

Bold and Brilliance

"Timidity does not inspire bold acts."
Mae Jemison

As a young and upcoming leader, I was blessed with naivety, that served well in "going for it." When we're not encumbered by other people's limits and constraints, we can step boldly into the work and be brilliant.

Step Into Your Ambition

Ambition is a double-edged sword. On one hand, it fuels you with the drive to push past your limits and achieve great things. On the other hand, it can be perceived as ruthless and selfish, leading to negative consequences in your personal and professional lives. Despite these potential drawbacks, I believe that ambition is an essential trait for success, both in dance and in leadership.

I was once told by a (well-meaning) colleague, "Well, you are ambitious, dear." The way she said it made me feel like it was a bad thing, something I should be ashamed of. But why? Why should we be ashamed of wanting to achieve great things, of striving for excellence? The truth is, we shouldn't. We should be proud of our ambition, and we should embrace it fully.

"I'm no longer available for feedback laced with someone else's limitations."

Of course, there are limits to how far we can push ourselves, and we must be mindful of the consequences of our actions. But this doesn't mean we should shy away from our ambition. Rather, we should step into it fully, embracing our goals and pursuing them with passion and determination.

In dance, ambition is a key driver of success. Dancers who are truly ambitious push themselves to their limits, both physically and mentally. They strive for perfection in their technique, their artistry, and their performance. They are always looking for ways to improve, to push past their boundaries, and to achieve greater heights.

Similarly, in leadership, ambition is essential. Leaders who are ambitious are constantly pushing themselves and their teams to do better. They set high standards and work tirelessly to achieve them. They are not content with mediocrity or complacency, but are always looking for ways to improve and to drive their organisations forward.

Ambition is not just about achieving personal success. It's also about making a positive impact on the world around us. Ambitious leaders are driven by a desire to make a difference, to leave a lasting legacy that will benefit others long after they're gone. They are not content with simply achieving their own goals; they want to help others achieve theirs as well.

So how can you step into your ambition fully? Here are five key steps:

1. Embrace your goals: Don't be afraid to set high standards for yourself. Embrace your ambition fully, and don't let anyone make you feel bad about it.

2. Work hard: Ambition without hard work is just a dream. If you want to achieve great things, you need to put in the time and effort required to make them happen.

3. Take risks: Ambition requires you to step outside your comfort zones and take risks. Be willing to try new things, to take on new challenges, and to push past your limits.

4. Be resilient: Ambition can be a bumpy road, with setbacks and failures along the way. But the most successful people are those who are able to pick themselves up and keep going, even in the face of adversity.

5. Help others: Remember that ambition is not just about achieving personal success. It's also about making a positive impact on the world around you. Look for ways to help others achieve their goals, and to make a difference in the world.

Ambition is a key driver of success in both dance and leadership. We should embrace our ambition fully, setting high standards for ourselves and working tirelessly to achieve them. But we must also be mindful of the impact our actions have on others, and strive to make a positive difference in the world around us. By stepping into our ambition fully, we can achieve great things and leave a lasting legacy that will benefit others long after we're gone.

Connection

'Your vibe attracts your tribe"

One of my favourite ways to connect with people is from stage, and spark a different way of thinking. During one of my speaking engagements, I shared my keynote: Courageous Leadership in the Modern World. After the event, I had a few questions about something I'd spoken about. It was that the new era of leadership is more than engagement. Leaders need to be focusing on connection.

You've probably been hearing for years about the importance of staff engagement. There are engagement surveys, engagement implementation plans, engagement KPIs, and possibly engagement morning teas, etc.

More recently, and what I've been discussing with my clients, is that engagement is no longer enough. Engagement is ensuring there's work that matters. While having work that matters is important, there's more to it.

What people are really seeking, now and into the future, is that they belong within their team and business. They feel accepted. And that they matter.

You have probably heard the ol' "everyone is replaceable": to have a truly connected workplace, we need to understand the brilliance that individuality brings to a team, that each and everyone within the business does matter, is seen, and feels important.

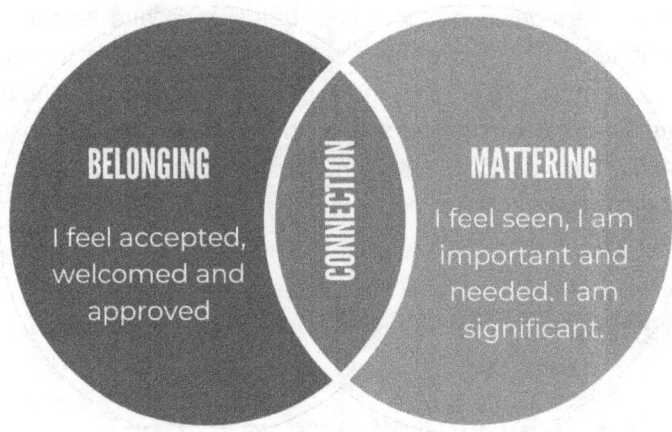

In order to create a thriving workplace that can survive the next three to five years (and beyond), it is essential to cultivate a culture of connection. The human element. And by that I mean creating a culture of belonging and mattering.

When employees feel connected to their work and to their colleagues, they are more likely to be engaged and productive. Additionally, a culture of connection fosters innovation and creativity.

Benefits of A Culture Of Connection

There are numerous benefits to creating a culture of connection in the workplace. First and foremost, when employees feel like they belong, they are more likely to be engaged and productive. Additionally, a culture of connection fosters innovation and creativity.

Here are some additional benefits of cultivating connection in the workplace:

1. Increased employee retention
    When employees feel connected to their work and to their colleagues, they are more likely to stick around (yes, please!).

    Employee turnover is expensive, not to mention the loss of knowledge and disruption to BAU, so reducing turnover is a top priority right now.

2. Improved communication
    A culture of connection encourages open communication between employees and leaders; this improved communication leads to better understanding and collaboration among team members, and across streams and divisions.

3. Greater job satisfaction
    Employees who feel like they belong are more likely to be satisfied with their jobs. A strong sense of connection is associated with increased satisfaction in all areas of life, not just work.

4. Enhanced well-being:
    A workplace of connection has been linked with enhanced well-being in employees. Studies have shown that employees who feel like they belong are more likely to report higher levels of physical and mental health.

Creating a culture of connection, belonging, and mattering in the workplace has numerous benefits for both employees, leaders, and employers alike. When employees feel connected to their work and their colleagues, they are more likely to be engaged and productive. Additionally, a culture of connection enhances communication, collaboration, retention rates, job satisfaction, and employees well-being. Implementing policies and practices that foster a sense of connection can go a long way towards creating a thriving workplace.

Build Advisory Panel

If you want to go fast go along, if you want to go far, go together—African Proverb.

Robin Dunbar; an Evolutionary anthropologist suggests there is a cognitive limit to the ideal number of people you can maintain stable social relationships. Meaning the relationships you build around you are important to your success.

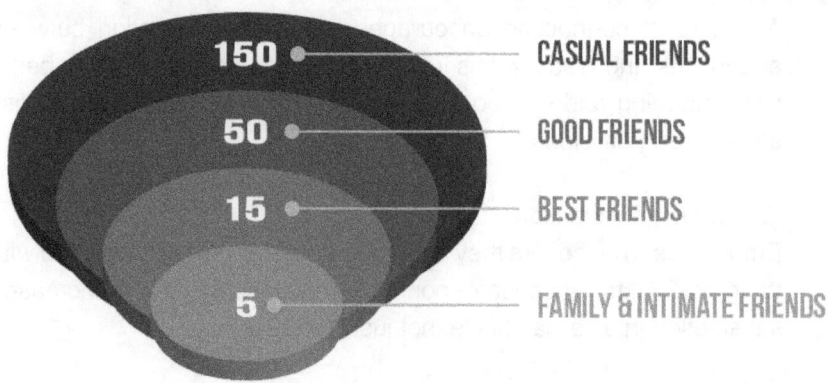

Start with your inner circle, the five closest relationships, these may be family or friends.

Beyond the inner circle is very important for leaders, this is the circle of 15. These are 15 key relationships that everybody needs. These are strong, robust relationships that become your core go-to people—your advisory panel. These are the people that have real impact on your success.

Who is on your advisory panel? Who do you need to add to your advisory panel?

The 50 good friends are those we can cognitively keep track of. These are people we enjoy spending time with, but wouldn't necessary consider them as people we would seek intimate advice from.

The 150 are those people we know through our broader communities. They're an extended network, and again not those who we would normally seek out for advice.

Be the Lighthouse

If you've previously heard one of my keynotes, I talk about *"being the lighthouse."* I reference the famous Jean Guichard picture; The French Lighthouse of La Jument which captures a moment Lighthouse keeper Theodore Malgorne came out to investigate the overhead helicopter where photographer Jean Guichard was taking photos during a raging storm. The picture was captured moments before the keeper retreated into safety as a mega wave crashed over the lighthouse. If you haven't seen the picture, check it out here www.gruntgritandgrace.com .

As a leader, you have a choice. You can stand strong and withstand the chaos. You can be a beacon of light and direction during this storm and uncertain time. **Or**, you can be the water and go with the current and the underlying panic.

Either way, you get to choose how you respond and how you react.

If you decide to be the lighthouse, here are some self-coaching questions you can ask yourself on how you can (literally) weather this storm and get your head in the game ready for your team.

1. Get clear on what is in your circle of control. What can you influence, what's beyond your circle of influence? And where are the gaps?

2. What's your focus for the next week? The next month? And what's your 90-day plan, to prepare and equip yourself?

3. Thinking directly of your team. **Who do you need to be** to show up for them? Who needs you on your a-game? Who are you responsible for?

4. In a time when *hashtag* vulnerability is the new black for leadership, are you ready to embrace it and be okay to not (yet) know what you don't know (and admit it to your team)?

5. What support are **you** going to require? Be articulate. If you're the lighthouse, you're going to need a strong foundation; what is your routine around self-care and resilience?

6. Lastly, remember, you always have a choice on how you react, and how you're going to respond.

Making It!

Knowing you've reached grace is a little bit like "it" being easy. It's fluid, you are comfortable in your own skin, your own capabilities, and you're comfortable in being uncomfortable!

You have uplifted your capability so much, there is now a new horizon, a new level of excellence, a deeper, bigger and better level that was previously inconceivable.

Before I had children, I was lucky (there's that word again) enough to be invited to join a group who were trekking for charity. The mission was to raise funds for some much-needed toilets for the north-western region of India, Chamba Valley. The problem was, the villagers who lived at the top of the hill would do their 'business', and as the rain fell the water naturally trailed down the mountain in to the river which was also the water source for the villagers at the bottom of the hill. Consequently, the people at the bottom of the hill were becoming increasingly unwell and sometimes dying from unsanitary water. Our team raised enough funds to be able to build multiple long drops throughout the Chamba Valley in the Himalaya. We also had the opportunity to trek the Himalayas to go and see these toilets. We were set to climb 4,000 metres above sea level; to give you some context, base camp is 5,364. In Adelaide where we were training the highest point is 759 metres above sea level.

After months and months of trekking training and putting miles in our legs it was time to start our trek. Each day was glorious and spectacular, and gruelling and exhausting. When we were in the valleys of the Himalaya it was warm and tropical, as we reached a peak, it was cold and snow-capped. Each day we'd set off for the peak of the mountain thinking we'd finally made it to 4,000 metres above sea level, only to arrive there to make camp and there was another peak waiting for us for the next day. You couldn't see this peak without climbing the previous one.

I often think about that trip when working with clients who are feeling like they're not sure what's next like they've reached their peak. However, with a little bit of grace, and a lot of grunt and grit, there's an even more spectacular view waiting for them from the peak of the next mountain they're climbing. Often we can't possibly conceive what's next while we're stuck in the moment.

Leading with grace is recognising that *"I have the bandwidth for the next challenge!"*

Reaching the pinnacle of grace is a remarkable achievement. It's a state of being where everything seems effortless and you are at ease with your own abilities, even when you're outside your comfort zone.

But there is always a new horizon to conquer, a new level of excellence to strive for. With every challenge comes the opportunity to grow and expand your capabilities, to build a bigger and better team that was once unimaginable.

I fondly remember my trek in the Himalayas, where each day brought its own unique challenges and breathtaking views. We climbed peaks that we never thought were possible. It was a gruelling and exhausting journey, but we kept going, driven by our determination and perseverance.

Leading with grace is like climbing a mountain. It requires hard work, dedication, and a willingness to push yourself to your limits. But with every step you take, you get closer to the summit, and the view from the top is truly spectacular.

As leaders, we must recognise that there is always more to achieve, more to learn, and more to do. It's about having the courage to step outside your comfort zone, embrace new challenges, and continue growing.

Leading with grace means having the bandwidth for the next challenge. It means being open to new ideas, being empathetic to your team, and leading with integrity. It's about being kind and compassionate, but also firm and decisive.

So, let us strive to reach new heights with grace. Let us be inspired by the breathtaking views that await us at the summit, and let us continue to push ourselves to be the best leaders we can be.

LESSON 19:

It's not always what you know, but it almost always is who you know. If you haven't started building your network already, today is the best day. Opportunities come from some of the most unexpected places. You may as well put yourself in the slipstream of opportunity.

I'd love to connect with you! I hang out mostly on LinkedIn. You can find me here - https://www.linkedin.com/in/ally-nitschke

The Finale

Hey there reader, Thank you.

You've made it this far, I hope this book as served as a resounding call to arms for you and leaders just like you in the ever-evolving business landscape. This is a manifesto for those who seek not just success, but enduring excellence. Throughout these pages, we've delved into the very essence of what it means to embody and lead with determination, persistence, agility and an unrelenting pursuit of brilliance

As a leader, you are charged with the responsibility to navigate uncharted waters, to confront challenges head-on, and to inspire greatness, not only in yourself but for those you lead, and those who follow.

This book has underscored the crucial role of 'Grunt' the story of unwavering determination that propels each of us forward, even when the odds are stacked against us.

By implementing the ideas and lessons in this book, you can expect to experience a positive transformation in your leadership commitment and outlook, both in the short term and long term. You will have gained a deeper understanding of your own capabilities, what you are comfortable with (and what you're not). You will be better equipped to handle challenges, create stronger teams and build meaningful relationships with your colleagues, peers, and stakeholders.

We have explored the concept of "Grit' the tenacity to endure and the resilience to persevere through adversity. It reminds us that true leaders do not waver in the face of setbacks. They rise stronger, more resilient and ready to embrace the next challenge.

The importance of 'Grace' in leadership has been a recurring theme – the ability to maintain composure, to inspire trust, and foster unity. It is a reminder that leadership is not just about achieving personal goals, but rather about creating a culture of connection, collaboration, respect and shared success.

Ultimately, my hope for you is that the energy, motivation and inspiration that comes from reading Grunt, Grit and Grace has illuminated the path to not only *doing* more, but *being* more as a leader. It challenges us to reach beyond the ordinary, to strive for brilliance, and to lead with purpose and passion.

You're aiming to be a 23%er after all.

It is a testament to the enduring power of the human spirit and the boundless potential of those who dare to leader with all their heart.

As we conclude this Journey together, may you, dear reader, and courageous leader, carry forward some of these lessons, and perhaps reflect on your own.

With Grunt, Grit and Grace as your guide, you are poised to not only lead your organisations to new heights but also to inspire a legacy of excellence that will ensure for year to come.

Go ahead, Eat the frog, get the worm, be the bird and soar!

About the Author

Ally Nitschke is a unique and awe-inspiring woman. She is also the brilliantly creative mind behind this groundbreaking leadership book, based on her own experiences applying the ethos of Grunt, Grit and Grace.

But while her place in the leadership, communication and speaking landscape might seem assured now, this was not always the case. Back in 2018, following a successful 15-year career in corporate leadership, and after the birth of her fourth child, Ally took a bold step. She left her career behind to launch "Made for More" a leadership and communication consultancy.

Saying goodbye to a secure paycheck, Ally set out to combine her own lived experiences, knowledge and values with extensive research, to tackle the many leadership and communication challenges she'd experienced in the corporate world for so long. Put simply, Ally believed we could all lead and communicate better.

With that message at her core, she built an idea to "be more, do more, achieve more" into a successful business, gradually gaining a foothold in the Australian and then international market. She has now spent the past 5 years delivering her own brand of leadership and communication training, frameworks, and programs across the globe.

In recent years, Ally has achieved remarkable success as a speaker through her authenticity, humour and clarity of message, winning the prestigious Kerrie Nairn Scholarship from the Professional Speakers Association, which recognises the most talented recent speaker in the Australian market.

Her first award winning book, Rise of the Courageous Leader, followed in 2022. And since it's release Ally is regularly sought for her captivating keynote speeches, to both Australian and international audiences, for executive coaching to help leaders achieve their best, and to create transformative leadership programs across a range of industries.

Ally came from quite humble beginnings, growing up on her parents' farm in the Adelaide Hills. This is where her late father instilled the values of hard work, humility, determination and kindness, which shaped Ally's success as a compassionate leader. On the other hand, Ally's mother, a pioneer in scientific research, imparted on her the power of both knowledge and independence as a woman - fuelling Ally's pursuit to make an impact in the corporate world.

At the heart of Ally's career journey across the complex worlds of finance, mergers, or government and business transformation, has been her ability to make things happen. From her early days working in retail banking, she has always felt a sense of comfort interacting with any customer, peer, or leader, both openly and honestly. Ally transcends the invisible personal boundaries many of us see, feel or perhaps fear within our workplace, which means she can speak as fluently and connectedly to a frontline team as she can to heads of a Department or your CEO.

When Ally's not demonstrating her grace on the corporate stage, she is most comfortable at home with her husband, Alex, and their four young boys. Ally's favourite sanctuary has always been her nearest beach, where she finds grounding, serenity, and a deep connection with her family. It's on these many beach days, gripping her toes into the soft sand, or playing with her boys in the ocean's waves, that Ally reflects on what brings us joy and connection, and that which inspires her to write, create and coach.

Working With Ally

In the realm of leadership development, a select few individuals truly shine as experts in their field, and Ally Nitschke undoubtedly belongs to this esteemed group. Her reputation, forged through years of experience and a profound grasp of leadership, communication, and personal growth, positions her as a guiding beacon for those aspiring to elevate their leadership prowess, enhance communication skills, and realise their utmost potential. Ally's profound impact extends across various avenues, including one-on-one coaching, transformative programs, workshops, masterclasses, and her illuminating "Made For More" podcast.

Collaborating with Ally is an invitation to embark on a transformative voyage toward leadership excellence. Through her personalised coaching, transformative programs, interactive workshops, engaging masterclasses, and the enlightening insights shared on her "Made For More" podcast, Ally empowers both individuals and organisations to soar to unprecedented heights of success. Her unwavering dedication to aiding others in uncovering their full potential and evolving into the leaders they are destined to be is what distinguishes Ally as a genuine luminary in the expansive realm of leadership development and communication.

![Ally Nitschke]

The Power of One-on-One Coaching

Ally Nitschke's one-on-one coaching sessions are a unique and personalised experience that individuals seeking growth and development crave. With a deep commitment to understanding her clients' unique needs, goals, and challenges, Ally guides them through a journey of self-discovery and empowerment. Her coaching style is marked by empathy, active listening, and the ability to ask the right questions that provoke profound insights.

In these sessions, Ally leverages her extensive expertise in leadership and communication to help clients overcome obstacles, break through self-imposed limitations, and cultivate the skills necessary for effective leadership. Whether you're a seasoned executive looking to refine your leadership approach or an emerging leader eager to build a strong foundation, Ally's one-on-one coaching can be a game-changer.

For more information, head to: www.madeformore.com.au/coaching-and-mentoring

Transformational Programs Engaging Workshops and Masterclasses

Ally Nitschke is renowned for her transformational programs, which are designed to bring about lasting change and growth in individuals and organisations. These programs delve deep into various aspects of leadership, communication, and personal development, providing participants with the tools, strategies, and insights needed to excel in their roles.

What sets Ally's transformational programs apart is her holistic approach. She recognizes that leadership is not just about skills but also about mindset and self-awareness. Through a combination of workshops, exercises, and coaching, participants in her programs gain a comprehensive understanding of their leadership potential and how to unlock it. Whether it's enhancing emotional intelligence, refining communication, or fostering a growth mindset, Ally's transformational programs leave a profound impact.

For more information, head to: www. madeformore.com.au/programs

Ally's workshops and masterclasses are dynamic and interactive experiences that draw upon her vast knowledge and engaging teaching style. These sessions are designed to be both informative and practical, offering participants actionable takeaways that can be immediately applied in their professional lives.

In her workshops, Ally covers a wide range of topics, from effective leadership strategies to advanced communication techniques. She creates an open and inclusive environment where participants can learn, practice, and receive feedback. Ally's ability to connect with her audience and simplify complex concepts makes her workshops and masterclasses highly sought after by individuals and organisations alike.

For more information, head to: www. madeformore.com.au/programs

Made For More Podcast

Ally Nitschke's influence extends beyond coaching and workshops to the digital realm through her "Made For More" podcast. This podcast is a treasure trove of insights, featuring interviews with prominent thought leaders, industry experts, and successful individuals who have unlocked their potential.

Each episode of the "Made For More" podcast is a journey of discovery, where Ally and her guests explore the various facets of leadership, personal growth, and communication. Listeners gain access to valuable advice, real-life stories, and practical tips that inspire and empower them to strive for greatness in their own lives.

Find the podcast on your favourite streaming services or head to www.madeformore.com.au/podcast

Not All Leadership Consultants Are Created Equal

There's no doubt that there are leadership experts on nearly every corner.

There are few that have been in significant leadership roles historically that can navigate the complexities of leadership today. Ally's extensive 20-year experience has seen her lead wonderful teams, terrible teams, and downright toxic and dysfunctional teams.

She has led small teams, and large teams of 500+. She has led complex and highly charged mergers, navigated transformational programs and has had some astounding results.

When Ally works with leaders and partners with organisations, she shares her hands-on experience from years of being in the trenches rather than relying on concepts and models of outdated leadership ideals.

Ally also brings global wisdom captured through working intimately with clients and a diverse range of industries.

Ally invests significantly in her own professional development year after year to maintian being at the forefront of leadership development globally to support her clients best.

Need an Engaging, Experienced World-class Speaker For Your Next Live or Virtual Event?

Ally has delivered 100s of keynote presentations, workshops, webinars and programs. She has presented in 35+ industries.

Ally is a Practical, Pragmatic and Personal speaker who weaves stories throughout her presentations, with humour, and energy that leave audiences inspired and ready for action.

Audiences have loved these topics
- Courageous Leadership in the modern world (the future of leadership)
- Welcoming GenZ to the workforce
- Courageous Conversations - the $104B problem we're keeping silent on
- The Future of leadership 2025 and beyond
- The importance of Boundaries and saying No

To see Ally's most up-to-date topics, head to
www.madeformore.com.au/speaking
To book Ally email hello@madeformore.com.au

199

Are you looking for the perfect gift for your Staff or to add to your swag bag at your next event for delegates

Ally's books are often bought in bulk where they are used as gifts and additional resources, and part of a promotional campaign, incentives and event gifts.

If you're looking for the ideal gift for your business customers, Ally's books are one of the most valuable presents you could possibly purchase.

There are all kinds of ways to add bulk book purchased from special print runs (with bespoke notes from global CEOs), your company messages printed in the book, through to including your company or event logo on the cover.

If this sounds like the ideal opportunity for your organisation, please email Ally's team at Hello@madeformore.com.au

Would You Like to Interview Ally Nitschke?

Over the last 5 years Ally has been interviewed many times across all types of media in Australia and internationally. She is very comfortable being interviewed for television and radio as much as being interviewed for features in a publication or to appear on a podcast show.

Ally can talk with great authority on the following:

- Courageous Leadership
- Courageous Conversations
- Difficult personalities
- The Future of Leadership
- The importance of Boundaries and saying no
- Moving Employer to place maker through belonging and mattering
- Self-Leadership and accountability
- Team leadership
- Navigating, leading and managing Change.
- Leading yourself as an entrepreneur

To see Ally's most upto date topics head to www.madeformore.com.au/speaking

Glossary

Ballet term Pronunciation	Description
Pas de Deux *Pa-de-der*	The dance of two. Often danced between the principal female and male dancers.
Port des Bras *Poor de bra*	Carriage of the arms. The movement of arms through various positions.
Barre *Bar*	Long stationery handrail, sometimes attached to the wall, sometimes freestanding. Used at the beginning of class to warm up and stretch on.
Pirouette *Pi-row-et*	The act of spinning on one foot, typically with the raised foot touching the knee of the supporting leg.
Fouetté *F-we-tay*	"whipped turning"), a spectacular turn in ballet, usually performed in series, during which the dancer turns on one foot while making fast outward and inward thrusts of the working leg at each revolution.
Corps-de-ballet *Cor-D-ballet*	the group of dancers who are not principal dancers or soloists.
Jete *Jet-aye*	A running split leap suspended in the air.

The Quintessential Foot Positions

★ ⭐ ★

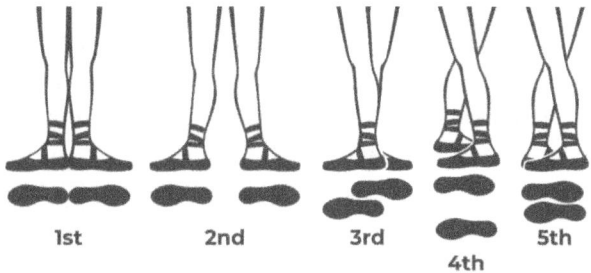

1st   2nd   3rd   5th

4th

Embarking on your ballet journey requires a solid foundation, and what better way to start than by acquainting yourself with the fundamental foot positions? These positions serve as the cornerstone of ballet technique.

Among the initial lessons in a novice ballet class, the five basic positions take precedence as they form the essence of classical ballet techniques, with nearly every step commencing and culminating in one of these positions.

The basic positions primarily concern the alignment and placement of the feet, aptly named as follows: first position, second position, third position, fourth position, and fifth position.

Understanding the basic positions is a great place to start when beginning your practice, since they make up the building blocks of ballet:

The five basic positions are usually one of the first things taught in a beginner's ballet class but are essential to the technique of classical ballet as practically every step begins and ends in one of the five basic positions.

First position: The heels are together with the toes of each foot pointed out toward either side, with legs straight and turned out, following the position of the feet.

Second position: Legs are straight, and the feet are turned out to each side like in first position, but the difference is that the heels do not touch and are instead about hip-width apart.

Third position: This position is rarely used, since it can be mistaken for a sloppy first or fifth position, but it is still important to learn, as it's the transition to fifth position in those formative years. Imagine being in first position, and then slide the heel of one foot so it lines up with the middle of the other foot (the arch), keeping both feet pointing out in opposite directions.

Fourth position: Stand with one foot about a foot's length in front of your other foot. Each foot should be pointing in an opposite direction, and the toes of the back foot should line up with the heel of the front foot.

Fifth position: This position is the most difficult one. It's like fourth position, but there is no gap between your feet. The toes of each foot should be directly in front of the heel of the other foot, and make sure your legs are turned out and straight.

The Classic Tale of *Cinderella*

★ ★ ★

The classic ballet of Cinderella first originated in 1813, which is the story of a young woman named Cinderella. Set in three acts, the story unfolds with Cinderella enduring the mistreatment of her stepmother and stepsisters. While they prepare for the Palace Ball, Cinderella remains behind, finding solace in her dreams and a portrait of her late mother.

Enter an unexpected guest, an old beggar woman, who recognises Cinderella's resemblance to her mother and presents her with the cherished portrait. In a remarkable turn of events, the beggar woman reveals herself as a beautiful Fairy Godmother. With a wave of her wand, she creates a magical forest, bestows Cinderella with glass slippers, and transforms a pumpkin and lizards into a majestic coach and horses.

Empowered by the Fairy Godmother's enchantment, Cinderella arrives at the Palace Ball, capturing the attention of the Prince himself. As they dance, their connection deepens, but the clock strikes midnight, signalling the end of the magic. Cinderella flees the ball, leaving behind a glass slipper, the only trace of her presence.

Act III brings us back to Cinderella's humble kitchen, where she cherishes the memory of the ball. However, her secret is discovered when the Prince and his entourage arrive, seeking the owner of the lost glass slipper. Each stepsister tries in vain to fit the slipper, but Cinderella, hidden away, produces the other slipper. The Prince recognises her and asks for her hand in marriage, and Cinderella forgives her stepmother and stepsisters.

In a final breathtaking scene, the kitchen transforms into a magical glade, where Cinderella and her Prince dance a romantic pas de deux. This pas de deux symbolises the union of their hearts and souls. As the guests celebrate the betrothal of Cinderella and the Prince, the guests return to celebrate their new princess, marking the beginning of a joyous chapter in Cinderella's life.

This timeless tale teaches us valuable lessons about leadership. From Cinderella's unwavering determination to her ability to rise about adversity.

Wear Sunscreen –
Everybody's free

* ⭐ *

Ladies and gentlemen of the class of '99
Wear sunscreen
If I could offer you only one tip for the future, sunscreen would be it
A long-term benefits of sunscreen have been proved by scientists
Whereas the rest of my advice has no basis more reliable
Than my own meandering experience, I will dispense this advice now.
Enjoy the power and beauty of your youth, oh, never mind
You will not understand the power and beauty of your youth
Until they've faded, but trust me, in 20 years, you'll look back
At photos of yourself and recall in a way you can't grasp now
How much possibility lay before you and how fabulous you really looked
You are not as fat as you imagine
Don't worry about the future
Or worry, but know that worrying
Is as effective as trying to solve an algebra equation by chewing bubble
gum
The real troubles in your life
Are apt to be things that never crossed your worried mind
The kind that blindsides you at 4 p.m. on some idle Tuesday
Do one thing every day that scares you.
Saying, don't be reckless with other people's hearts
Don't put up with people who are reckless with yours
Floss
Don't waste your time on jealousy

Sometimes you're ahead, sometimes you're behind
The race is long and, in the end, it's only with yourself
Remember compliments you receive, forget the insults
If you succeed in doing this, tell me how
Keep your old love letters, throw away your old bank statements
Stretch
Don't feel guilty if you don't know what you want to do with your life
The most interesting people I know
Didn't know at 22 what they wanted to do with their lives
Some of the most interesting 40-year-olds I know still don't
Get plenty of calcium
Be kind to your knees
You'll miss them when they're gone.
Maybe you'll marry, maybe you won't
Maybe you'll have children, maybe you won't
Maybe you'll divorce at 40, maybe you'll dance the "Funky Chicken."
On your 75th wedding anniversary
Whatever you do, don't congratulate yourself too much.
Or berate yourself either.
Your choices are half-chance, so are everybody else's.
Enjoy your body, use it every way you can.
Don't be afraid of it or what other people think of it.
It's the greatest instrument you'll ever own.
Dance, even if you have nowhere to do it but your own living room.
Read the directions even if you don't follow them.
Do not read beauty magazines, they will only make you feel ugly.
Get to know your parents, you never know when they'll be gone for good
Be nice to your siblings, they're your best link to your past
And the people most likely to stick with you in the future.
Understand that friends come and go
But a precious few, who should hold on.
Work hard to bridge the gaps in geography and lifestyle
For as the older you get
The more you need the people you knew when you were young
Live in New York City once but leave before it makes you hard
Live in northern California once but leave before it makes you soft.

Travel
Accept certain inalienable truths
Prices will rise, politicians will philander, you too, will get old
And when you do, you'll fantasize that when you were young
Prices were reasonable, politicians were noble
And children respected their elders.
Respect your elders.
Don't expect anyone else to support you
Maybe you have a trust fund, maybe you'll have a wealthy spouse
But you never know when either one might run out.
Don't mess too much with your hair
Or by the time you're 40 it will look 85.
Be careful whose advice you buy but be patient with those who supply it
Advice is a form of nostalgia, dispensing it is a way of fishing the past
From the disposal, wiping it off, painting over the ugly parts
And recycling it for more than it's worth.
But trust me on the sunscreen.

Notes

Notes

Notes

Notes

Notes

Notes